# THE STRONG-WILLED WIFE

Using Your Personality
to Honor God and
Your Husband

Debbie L. Cherry, PhD

D0067036

## NAV PRESS®

x

BRINGING TRUTH TO LIFE

The Navigators is an international Christian organization. Our mission is to advance the gospel of Jesus and His kingdom into the nations through spiritual generations of laborers living and discipling among the lost. We see a vital movement of the gospel, fueled by prevailing prayer, flowing freely through relational networks and out into the nations where workers for the kingdom are next door to everywhere.

NavPress is the publishing ministry of The Navigators. The mission of NavPress is to reach, disciple, and equip people to know Christ and make Him known by publishing life-related materials that are biblically rooted and culturally relevant. Our vision is to stimulate spiritual transformation through every product we publish.

www.navpress.com

NAVPRESS, BRINGING TRUTH TO LIFE, and the NAVPRESS logo are registered trademarks of NavPress. Absence of ® in connection with marks of NavPress or other parties does not indicate an absence of registration of those marks.

ISBN-10: 1-60006-090-0
ISBN-13: 978-1-60006-090-8

Cover design by Tim Green / The Designworks Group www.thedesignworksgroup.com
Cover photo by Steve Gardner, www.shootpw.com

Creative Team: Terry Behimer, Karen Lee-Thorp, Darla Hightower, Arvid Wallen, Kathy Guist

Some of the anecdotal illustrations in this book are true to life and are included with the permission of the persons involved. All other illustrations are composites of real situations, and any resemblance to people living or dead is coincidental.

Unless otherwise identified, all Scripture quotations in this publication are taken from the HOLY BIBLE: NEW INTERNATIONAL VERSION® (NIV®). Copyright © 1973, 1978, 1984 by International Bible Society. Used by permission of Zondervan Publishing House. All rights reserved. Other versions used include: the *King James Version* (KJV).

Cherry, Debbie L.
 The strong-willed wife : using your personality to honor God and your husband / Debbie L. Cherry.
  p. cm.
 Includes bibliographical references.
 ISBN 1-60006-090-0
 1. Wives--Religious life. 2. Submissiveness--Religious aspects--Christianity. I. Title.
 BV4528.15.C44 2007
 248.8'435--dc22

2006030794

Printed in the United States of America

1 2 3 4 5 6 7 8 / 11 10 09 08 07

This book is dedicated to my husband, Jim.
Thank you for being the most
loving and patient husband any
strong-willed wife could ever ask for!

# Contents

CHAPTER 1
Strong Willed? Who, Me?                                    1

CHAPTER 2
Are You a Strong-Willed Wife?                             9

CHAPTER 3
But God Made Me This Way, Didn't He?                     23

CHAPTER 4
Where Personality Comes From                            31

CHAPTER 5
Culture vs. God's Pattern for Marriage                  45

CHAPTER 6
How Positive Traits Can Turn Negative                   61

CHAPTER 7
The Strong-Willed Woman Chooses a Man                   77

CHAPTER 8
Rights and Responsibilities                             95

CHAPTER 9
As Christ Loved the Church: A Husband's
Responsibilities                                       113

CHAPTER 10
As to the Lord: A Wife's Responsibilities 131

CHAPTER 11
The Myths About Submission 145

CHAPTER 12
Real Submission 161

CHAPTER 13
Why Won't I Let Him Lead? 179

CHAPTER 14
I Don't Feel Like Submitting Today! 201

CHAPTER 15
How to Relinquish Control 217

CHAPTER 16
What If My Husband Won't Lead? 237

CHAPTER 17
Celebrating Each Other's Strengths 253

Notes 261

About the Author 263

# CHAPTER 1

# Strong Willed? Who, Me?

THE NEED FOR THIS book hit me several years ago while I was attending a convention in Nashville. I had skipped a couple of sessions to spend time with an old friend, David. We talked for what seemed like hours about how God has blessed each of us. We eventually got around to talking about our relationships, and he shared with me some of his struggles in his marriage. He felt he could never do anything right, could never please his wife, could seldom make suggestions or give advice that she received well, and he definitely did not feel like the leader in his home.

Now, David has never been the power-hungry, control-seeking type. He wasn't saying, "She won't do what I tell her to do!" He simply said he didn't feel like the man of the house. He felt discouraged and ineffective. He described his wife as having a "very strong personality." He said he liked that she was an independent thinker and was driven to accomplish so much. That was part of what attracted him to her to begin with. He was proud of who she was and what she did, but he didn't feel she respected or needed him. He felt that they weren't a team.

Because we had been friends for so long, David also

knew how very strong my personality is and hoped for some insight as to how my husband and I have worked out a healthy balance.

As I listened to him describe Renee, I realized he just as easily could have been describing me. And then I wondered whether Jim experienced some of these same feelings. Did he feel he wasn't allowed to be the head of our home? Did he feel disrespected and not needed? Was he frustrated that I questioned his decisions? I didn't know. I had seldom evaluated our marriage from this perspective, and then only briefly, because I didn't like what I saw. I determined to learn how Jim felt.

When I called home that evening, Jim answered my questions honestly. We both realized we had been ignoring some significant issues. We also realized how many marriages we knew of (now that we thought about it) that were suffering from the same phenomenon.

As Jim and I talked, my mind was spinning with the idea of writing about the impact strong-willed personalities have on marriages everywhere. We talked about strong-willed women and how they are changing the way marriages look today. Before we hung up the phone, Jim suggested that we pray about and seriously consider writing a book together: *The Strong-Willed Couple.* He even wrote that title on a Post-It note and stuck it to his computer. (It's still there—I think more as a reminder than as a thorn in my side.)

I immediately wrote down my thoughts. I spent the rest of the conference inspired, and by the time I got home, I couldn't wait to tell Jim all about the book *I* was going to write, called *Taming the Strong-Willed Wife.* I had moved from writing a book together to taking over and deciding how I would do it. Any guesses just how strong willed I really am?

## IS THIS MESSAGE REALLY NEEDED?

I keep receiving confirmation about how much this book is needed. Pastors tell me of marriages in their congregations struggling with this issue. And being a marriage and family therapist, I am met in my office almost every day by couples who are showing the damage that results when a wife's strong will doesn't honor God or her husband. Everywhere I turn, I see topsy-turvy signs where the couple isn't following God's plan but wonders why their relationship doesn't work.

When I feel exceptionally brave, I tell people about writing this book. I get all kinds of reactions. Husbands and pastors say, *"Please* write that book; it is so needed." But I get a totally different reaction from other strong-willed wives. Their looks say more than words could convey. The utter contempt and "How dare you!" are branded into my mind. I explain that the book is not about telling wives they're wrong (I know better than that), but just about figuring out how to balance wills within our marriages. Still, many women have made up their minds that I'm a traitor. That's one reason I've resisted writing this: I've doubted myself.

I have realized over time that, like many of these women, I was not nearly as resistant to the concept of submission as I was to the idea of someone telling me there is something inherently wrong with my personality. I think many of us strong-willed wives believe that a strong will and submission are extreme opposites, and we can't have both. So anytime someone challenges us to be submissive, we think they are telling us to change who we are. They're saying our strong will is sinful.

I don't believe we have made this up in our heads either. I think the term *strong willed* has been given a bad rap.

3

Those of us with strong personalities feel judged because of the negative actions of some strong-willed women. We are tired of hearing about what's wrong with our personalities and how we should change if we want to glorify God. God made us this way, didn't He? So why do our personalities seem so contrary to His Word? And why do we feel like we don't fit in?

As a result of all this negative press about strong personalities, we strong-willed wives often want to focus only on our positive traits—and there are many. But inside we know that some of these traits are not so positive and can harm our relationships if allowed to continue unchecked. Many of us feel insecure, especially when it comes to fitting in and looking like a "good Christian wife."

## "I JUST DON'T FIT IN!"

I gave up trying to fit in many years ago. I decided some part of me was broken and could never be fixed. I would never be as good a Christian as my seemingly submissive, quiet counterparts. I thought I was the only wife out there who quickly volunteered to work in the church nursery when I saw the Sunday sermon topic was biblical submission. Why would I want to hear some man preach on the verses I avoided at all cost? I knew I couldn't reconcile them with my personality.

I believe God knit me together in my mother's womb. I believe He placed inside of me these strong passions to do something great for Him. I believe He gave me the intellect and drive I needed to make these desires a reality. So if God put all these things in me, why should I feel guilty for having them? Why would I feel like less of a Christian and like a poor wife when I demonstrated these God-given traits?

Over time the conflict between my strong will and my definition of a "good Christian wife" became too heavy to carry, and I decided I had to let go of one or the other. Any guesses which one I gave up? That's right: the harder one.

I loved how it felt to accomplish much, to make decisions and be in charge, to have people look to me for direction. All of that came naturally to me. My strong-willed personality served me well and gained me many compliments outside my home. I felt good about myself and my accomplishments. So if I could keep only one of these sides of myself, I chose to keep the one that made me feel good (at least most of the time). The part of me that had continued to try to be a good Christian wife was already feeling defeated and hopeless. It was obvious that I was failing more often than not at that ideal of being a submissive, quiet, supportive wife. So I decided to use my refined problem-solving skills to justify why I didn't need to be like all those other women. I used several different tactics to reduce this internal conflict:

- I used *selective blindness* when reading the Bible. I ignored problematic verses, passages, and commands.
- Several *psychological theories* worked for me to explain that God and others should not expect me to be different because I was "born this way."
- The idea of *unconditional love* convinced me that Jim liked me just the way I was and didn't need or even want me to be submissive.
- *Avoidance* was the key when it came to women's groups, conferences, marital small groups, sermons, and books that might challenge my thinking.

This all worked fairly well to keep the internal conflict at bay most of the time. But something didn't fit quite right, and I knew it. I didn't fit! I didn't fit anywhere in my world. I didn't fit with the strong-willed women of the world; I wasn't a male-hating women's libber seeking to dominate everyone in her path. I did have strong convictions that I wanted to share, but they usually weren't about anything those women wanted to discuss.

I felt I didn't fit with most of the Christian women I encountered either. At least not the ones I considered to be good Christians. They all seemed to be doing everything by *the* Book. They were soft spoken and meek. They had gentle spirits and moldable hearts. They were servant hearted, submissive, and content to be in the background. I, on the other hand, was the extreme opposite. These were the women whom privately I viewed as weak and dependent, yet somewhere inside I felt jealous of them. I felt they were what God intended women to be, and I would never measure up. So why even try?

My strong will got stronger. To counter the feelings of inferiority regarding other Christian wives, I threw myself into my accomplishments. I worked hard and focused on helping marriages heal. I wrote books and taught couples to grow closer to each other and to God. How could anyone consider me inferior — look at all I could do?

I knew that if I wrote this book, I might not be well liked. How could any intelligent, strong-willed woman of today write such a thing? Was I really about to stand up and tell women to be submissive to their husbands? Did I understand submission enough to practice it in my own life? Was my strong will strong enough to sustain me through the controversy? How could I reconcile my God-given personality with obedience to His commands about marriage? And did I want to? I knew that I was in no way a submissive wife. I had no desire to become one either. I know that may sound awful, but I'm being honest with you.

I held very strong opinions (surprised?) about what submission was portrayed to be, and I believed God just didn't create me that way. I have always hated being told what to do. And you can multiply that by a thousand if what I'm being told to do is "be submissive." So I sure wasn't going to write a book telling wives they should be more submissive. No way! Not me!

**I SURRENDER**

But because the idea for this book kept drawing me back, I started researching submission in very small doses. I couldn't take too much at one time. Still, I knew that eventually I would have to come face-to-face with who I believed I was created to be and what God required of me as a Christian and as a wife. This book is the result of that conflict coming to a head and challenging me to be everything God intended me to be. The Holy Spirit wouldn't let this die. I have finally surrendered to learning about God's design for leadership within marriage, and I am even willing for Him to work in me to bring me under His plan for my marriage.

I am still not completely sure if this book was more for you or for me. Even now, I know I'm not living out all that I need to. I am simply practicing by responding to the Holy Spirit and, yes, *submitting* to writing this book. I pray that He will honor the effort and help me, along with you, learn the concepts presented here. I hope that as you read about my struggles and successes and those of many other women, you will be encouraged to be all God created you to be.

As I'm sure you can tell, this is not just a feel-good book to help us strong-willed wives embrace who we are expecting everyone else to accommodate us. Although accepting who we are is important—and we will discuss many positive traits God has blessed us with—that is not my primary focus. This book is a challenge to each of us to open ourselves up and let the Holy Spirit show us how He wants to use our personalities to bring honor to Himself and to our husbands. We won't lose who we are, and we won't get "fixed." I would resist that as much as you would. We just need to love our Savior even more than we thought possible through our obedience to His commands. We need to change our focus from ourselves to Christ and what He wants from us, and then use our strong will to accomplish that.

I hope you'll prayerfully consider how your personality may be affecting your relationship with your husband. If you are aware of difficulties in acting like a team within your marriage, or if you feel you are always the one in control or that there is a struggle for control, then I challenge you to turn the page and begin your journey.

## COMING UP NEXT

As we start this journey together, we will look at what a strong-willed wife is and whether you are one. I want you to identify and accept the many positive aspects of being strong willed. These traits can help us do wonderful things. It is important to keep a balance in how we look at ourselves, seeing the positive and the not-so-positive, but why not begin with what's great about being strong willed?

# CHAPTER 2

# Are You a Strong-Willed Wife?

AS I LOOKED AROUND my living room, I was amazed at the uniqueness of each woman sitting there. They had responded to my invitation to share their thoughts about being strong-willed wives. Although each of these women demonstrated strong-willed characteristics (thus the invitations), the similarities stopped there. They were different ages, from different backgrounds, with different life directions, and at different stages of life. There were two stay-at-home moms, a pastor's wife, a school teacher, a counselor, an accountant, and a college student, to name a few. They talked a mile a minute about how they had debated even coming. One said something like, "What's so wrong with being strong willed? Why does everyone have to think that's such a bad thing?"

As I asked them to settle down, I hoped to contain and direct these powerful, independent women at least enough to hear what each had to say. To address the statement I had just overheard, I explained that this was a brainstorming session and the first topic was "What's so great about being strong willed?" Immediately the atmosphere changed. I could almost see the electricity sparking between these bright minds. They were excited not only about brainstorming but even more about realizing that this was not another time when they would feel their strong will was a negative trait. One woman sighed and said, "I'm so glad someone understands that being strong willed can be good! I usually feel like I'm condemned for being so strong. I almost didn't come tonight because I wasn't sure I was in the mood to be labeled *strong willed* one more time. I've learned to hate that term."

Why do we bristle at the term *strong willed*? Is it really something to dread? I don't think so. I think just about every human being has some tendencies to be strong willed at some times in their lives. Even the most quiet and reserved wife and mother can stand up and take charge in times of crisis. She can reach deep inside herself and do what it takes to protect her family from pain or injustice. You back just about any mama bear into a corner, and she will come out fighting for the survival of herself and her cubs. In such situations, these traits are applauded. These action-oriented, determined, take-charge traits haven't given the negative image to being strong willed. But these are exactly the traits that get ignored in those of us who live this lifestyle every day.

So if any of us can show a strong-willed nature sometimes, what does it take to be considered a strong-willed wife in the sense that I am using? Those of us who are true strong-willed wives are passionate about what's happening or not happening around us. We live, breathe, eat, and sleep strong wills every day. We see the world not as something to react to but as something to impact. We look to make a change somewhere, anywhere. We have big dreams and are willing to do just about whatever it takes to make those dreams a reality. And sometimes we are even the ones who create the crisis that others around us then respond to.

Strong-willed wives have many positive traits that can

take us and those around us to the next level. But every one of these positive traits can become our downfall if we aren't careful. This personality type has both positive and negative traits just like every other personality style, but the positive traits have been overlooked when it comes to being strong, independent Christian women.

Maybe you have been told for years how your strong-willed nature is negative, unchristian, unladylike, and flat-out rebellious. Of course, you are intimately aware of the times and places that your strong will has gotten you into trouble or made relationships difficult. But you also know that there is so much more to you than those incidents. This chapter will help you identify if you are a strong-willed wife and the strengths this personality style affords you. Later on, in chapter 6, we'll look at how too much of even a good trait can turn negative and the importance of keeping our strong will subject to God.

## TAKING A LOOK AT YOURSELF

Before going any further, it is important to determine if you fit the profile of a strong-willed wife. I have heard the term misapplied to any woman who ever has an opinion of her own. And multiply that by 100 if her opinion happens to be opposite of or different from her husband's. This is *not* what I'm describing here. Wives can and do have opinions of their own all the time. God created all of us with brains that allow us to think for ourselves, make decisions, and manage our world. And just because we are able to do that does not make us strong willed. Be careful not to label yourself as strong willed just because you were told by your parents, teachers, or even your husband that you are. Instead, take the quiz below to identify where you fit on the continuum of being a strong-willed wife.

As you read the following statements, mark those that reflect how you think or act *most of the time*. No one will show any of these traits all the time, but consider how you respond in general. If you show that particular trait sometimes but rarely, then skip over it. But if you show the identified trait more days than not (more than 50 percent of the time), then mark it. Most important, be honest with yourself, even if the picture doesn't flatter you (not all our strong-willed traits are positive). And if you are really brave and looking for some insight into just how strong willed you are, copy this quiz and ask your husband to fill it out about you.

## Are You a Strong-Willed Wife?

☐ 1. I like to be the person in charge.

☐ 2. I am passionate and enthusiastic about the things I believe in strongly.

☐ 3. I am often directive in my interactions with my husband (for instance, I tell my husband what to say when he's on the phone, give him directions when driving, and so on).

☐ 4. I am persistent and persuasive in presenting my ideas.

☐ 5. I believe my way is the best or most efficient and expect others to agree.

☐ 6. I am not afraid to venture into the unknown. I see it as a challenge to try something new.

☐ 7. I have trouble trusting that my husband will do what I ask him to do.

☐ 8. When someone asks my husband a question, I jump in and answer for him.

☐ 9. I feel exhausted because I seem to be doing everything myself.

☐ 10. I often redo things my husband has done around the house.

☐ 11. I am quick to give my husband advice or suggestions about how I would do something, even if unsolicited.

☐ 12. I have strong opinions and convictions and like to share them.

☐ 13. I am a problem solver and am energized when working on problems others have been unable to solve.

☐ 14. I have a strong desire to make a difference in my world.

☐ 15. I am outgoing and enjoy standing out in a crowd.

☐ 16. I am willing to step out on a limb for something I believe in, even if it means conflict with those I love.

☐ 17. I resist being told what to do and will often do the opposite just because I can.

☐ 18. I become impatient with those around me when they don't think, move, or respond as fast as I do.

☐ 19. I have difficulty looking at my own mistakes but can be quick to point out the mistakes of others.

☐ 20. I am always looking for new challenges and adventures to help keep boredom at bay.

☐ 21. I am independent and like making my own decisions.

☐ 22. I am difficult to discourage and believe "nothing is impossible."

☐ 23. Speaking words such as "I'm sorry" or "I was wrong" feel like they will choke me.

☐ 24. I question my husband's decisions and require explanations for them.

☐ 25. I can't seem to back down in an argument even when I know I should.

☐ 26. I hate to be ignored, especially when I have something to say.

☐ 27. I engage in "verbal overkill" (otherwise known as nagging) and believe eventually others will see things my way.

☐ 28. "Obey" is a dirty four-letter word in my vocabulary.

☐ 29. I believe I shouldn't have to repeat myself.

☐ 30. I believe there is no such thing as "none of my business."

☐ 31. I dream big and believe I can do it all.

☐ 32. I hate to have to wait for anything and look for a way to move things along.

☐ 33. I'm more likely to explain than to admit if I'm wrong.

☐ 34. When there is chaos and things don't seem to be organized, I am quick to see how things could work better and to jump in and help fix them.

☐ 35. Once my mind is made up, I seldom deviate.

☐ 36. Life is a competition, and I'm going to win.

☐ 37. I use words such as "me," "my," and "mine" more than "we," "us," or "ours."

☐ 38. I hate to ask for help.

☐ 39. Little wrongs can often seem like huge injustices to me.

☐ 40. I can be very creative and resourceful when it comes to accomplishing my goals and solving problems.

So, do you know how you did? Total up your marks and let's see. Add one point for each statement marked.

If you scored less than 10 you can set this book down and relax. Pass it along to the friend who came to mind most often! Although you have some strong-willed traits, you are using them only when appropriate or absolutely necessary. As I said earlier, everyone can be strong willed when necessary.

Your strong-willed nature is likely to be evident only in times of crisis, when you feel backed into a corner, or when you feel passionately about a topic that needs to be addressed. But even in those situations, you may think twice and weigh the consequences before exerting yourself.

Scores of 11–25 indicate that you have a strong-willed nature that both you and those close to you are quite aware of. You likely think and act fast, have strong and passionate opinions, tackle several things at once, and are a take-charge woman. However, you likely are able to tone down or repress this strong will in situations where it seems appropriate to do so. You usually know when enough is enough and can back down when you need to (at least outwardly). You are able to let others be in charge when it's naturally their place to do so, but you are likely still giving suggestions from the sidelines. Your strong-willed nature both positively and negatively affects your relationships, especially your marriage, but you are likely struggling with many of the concepts that will be discussed here.

Scores of 26–40 are for those of us who would never be mistaken as anything less than strong willed. We wouldn't know how to tone down our strong will even if we wanted to (which usually we don't). Everyone knows when we are around. We are a force to be reckoned with. Our husbands may have long since given up trying to protect us or tell us to do or not do anything. And our friends have learned to shake their heads and roll their eyes, saying, "There she goes again." We are born leaders, dynamic and energetic, and seldom realize when we have just bowled right over someone who's moving slower than we are. We make quick decisions for both ourselves and those around us and rarely consider the consequence until after the action has been taken (and sometimes not even then). This book was written mainly for this highest scoring group, for we are the ones who struggle daily with these concepts.

## WHAT'S SO GREAT ABOUT BEING A STRONG-WILLED WOMAN?

The positive traits that go along with being strong willed are numerous and worth celebrating when they are present in healthy doses. A controlled strong will is a wonderful force that can bring benefits to just about everyone. But like many forces of nature, if it is not controlled, it can wreak havoc. Think about the power of fire. Small, contained doses benefit our lives tremendously. We can cook, get warm, and socialize around a controlled burn. But what happens when that same fire grows too big and too strong? What happens when the fire is no longer controlled and contained by its maker? Everyone runs for cover!

Your strong will is much like that fire. As long as it's controlled and contained by its Maker, it can benefit you and those you love. It can bring changes to the world and do amazing things for the kingdom of heaven. However, if your will does not remain subject to God, it can quickly rage out of control. When that happens, the devastation can be vast and the damage long standing. So, as we spend the rest of this chapter looking at the positive aspects of our strong-willed personality, I ask you to remember that the key to keeping our personality positive is having a healthy respect for the fire we hold inside. At any moment, what is good and healthy can turn destructive if left unattended. In order to keep that balanced focus, chapter 6 will discuss how these healthy traits can turn negative when left to run rampant.

As long as we commit ourselves and our personality style to God first, and then use these traits as needed to bring Him glory in all we do, then we can accept and celebrate being strong-willed wives.

## WHAT A STRONG WILL ISN'T

As strong-willed women we are often misunderstood and mislabeled. Because the term *strong willed* has become associated more with negative traits, I think the positive traits have become lost. Let's look at some of the labels that we may have to fight as we learn to accept the positive parts of our strong-willed nature.

*Strong-willed wives are not bad girls.*
For years a strong will was treated as synonymous with rebellion. Be honest. When you hear people in the workplace or at church describe a woman as strong willed, what do you think they're saying? Does their tone of voice, body language, or the context of the conversation tell you what they're thinking? I'm sure it does. And I'm even more certain it isn't positive. People generally mean some woman out there isn't doing what she should be doing or what everyone else is doing. So what? What's so wrong with being different and thinking outside the box? Who wants to be like everyone else anyway? We sure don't.

Strong-willed women are free thinkers. We move to our own drummer. But that doesn't have to translate into rebellion, although those around us who are more conforming and tend to obey without question may think so. The critical thinking and open questioning that we do are not sin. And just because we may be willing to go against the grain of society, and even our own churches, and stir things up a bit doesn't mean we are wrong. We are not conformists who are content to just sit back and let things be. We are movers and shakers who believe things can change for the better and are willing to help make those changes happen. Jesus was not a conformist. His presence on earth stirred things up and brought revolutionary change. Would you call Him rebellious or wrong? I don't think so.

Like our Savior, we often see things differently from those around us, and we want to see change. We believe in a better world and are willing to ruffle a few feathers to get there. We are born leaders with firm convictions and are willing to go to just about any length to make our dreams a reality. We are dynamic, charismatic, confident, outspoken, and independent. We are passionate about what we believe to be true and love an opportunity to share what we think with others. We don't see ourselves as rebellious as the world defines that term. But we are willing to rebel against the wrongs we see in this world and to fight hard for justice.

*Strong-willed wives are not the opposite of Christian.*
I hate that so many of us have believed we are less Christlike than our quiet counterparts. I have talked to women who admitted to doubting their salvation simply because of their personality style. Just for clarification, your salvation is a state of your heart and soul. It is based solely on your faith in our Lord Jesus Christ, not on how you feel today or how you view and interact with the world.

I believe we doubt our Christianity not because of conviction from the Holy Spirit but rather because of the condemnation of misled people around us. When church leaders portray a "good Christian wife" as quiet, meek, mild, and submissive, of course we will feel inadequate. We don't fit that mold. We are opinionated and assertive and love our Savior intensely. We are willing to stand up for what is right even if it means being labeled a troublemaker. We believe God created us equal, and that means we have thoughts, opinions, suggestions, and recommendations that need to be heard and considered just as any man's do. We are joint heirs with Christ and an equally important part of the body of Christ. We are able to stand alongside any Christian brother or sister and do the will of our Father. We don't shirk responsibility but rather welcome it.

We find a proud lineage in the Bible of women who were bold and committed followers of our God, including Queen Esther (book of Esther), Abigail (1 Samuel 25), Deborah (Judges 4–5), Rebekah (Genesis 24–28), Miriam (Exodus 2; 15; Numbers 12), Sarah (Genesis 11–23), Martha (Luke 10; John 11), and Priscilla (Acts 18). As you read about these women, you realize none of them is perfect. Each one of them had faults and showed not only positive traits of being strong willed but also some not-so-positive ones. But regardless, they all loved and served God just as we do.

*Strong-willed wives are not men haters.*
Being a strong-willed wife does not mean that we are on the rampage to rise above our husbands. We are not power-hungry women seeking to overthrow God's authority structure. We love our husbands; we just don't believe loving them means being seen and not heard.

As strong-willed wives, we desire to be equal partners working together in our home and family. We believe that our family can do more, be more, and serve more if we are working together to accomplish the tasks set before us. We love

Proverbs 31 and the woman represented there. She is who we believe we are or can be. We are problem solvers, and we trust our ability to make good decisions. We are determined, driven, persuasive, and focused when it comes to managing our homes, businesses, children, finances, and anything else before us. But that doesn't mean we want to do it alone or without our husbands' approval. We love it when a well-orchestrated plan comes together and both husband and wife are proud of who they are and what they can do. We don't get stuck in the ruts of conventional society that once defined a man and a woman by the jobs we can or should do. We are willing to think outside the box, evaluate our strengths and weakness as a couple, and then utilize each person's strengths to benefit the home.

## HOW DO YOU SEE YOURSELF NOW?

When God knit us together in our mother's womb, He didn't give us all these skills and passions just to have us hide them away. We are to use everything that our Creator blesses us with to bring Him glory. Are you using your strong will to glorify God? Are these positive traits evident in your daily life? Is the fruit you are showing a result of a personality style that is subject to God Almighty? Or are you allowing these traits to rage out of control and spoil the fruit that you want to produce?

Now that you are thinking of positive aspects of who you are, I encourage you to strengthen these and let them shine. As you accept and celebrate who you were created to be, it will be easier to keep these traits under control and with a positive focus.

**COMING UP NEXT**

Now that you have identified just how strong willed you are, and you're considering that being a strong-willed wife can be extremely positive, it's time to consider where your strong-willed personality came from. In the next two chapters, we will look at different sources that can create a strong will in us. I encourage you to be honest with yourself about how much of your strong will is really from God and how much may be the result of other influences.

# CHAPTER 3

# But God Made Me This Way, Didn't He?

AS YOU THINK ABOUT the strong-willed wives in the world today, you can likely picture several women you know personally. And if I asked you to describe these women, you would likely give similar descriptions of them. If we were able to take a slice of time out of more than one strong-willed wife's day, we would see similarities. But just because they look similar on the outside does not mean they are even close on the inside. The motivations behind the behaviors can be very different from one strong-willed wife to the next.

The inner core of why we act the way we do is as unique as our fingerprints. Still, a few main categories apply. This chapter will help you identify that inner core and the truth behind your motivations so you can better understand how your strong will developed and how much of it you should choose to keep.

## A TALE OF THREE WOMEN

Let's take a snapshot of the lives of three women as they look today. Liz, Sue, and Carrie are in their late thirties to early forties and have known each other for several years. They live in the same town and attend the same church, and they have all three identified themselves as strong-willed wives. Their church has planned an evening fellowship that does not include children. Let's look at how these three women prepare for tonight's event.

If we watch them in their separate environments simultaneously, we see how similar some of their basic behaviors are. The day of the event, Liz spends most of her time cleaning the whole house by herself before the babysitter arrives. Carrie instead requests her husband's aid in the housecleaning, but then checks everything she asked him to do. She even goes back over the kitchen cabinets after he finishes. Sue asks her husband to take care of the babysitter situation and then asks him repeatedly if he has done it and if he remembered to tell her _____ . And although all three of the husbands give the sitter instructions and phone numbers while their wives finish dressing, each of these women gives last-minute instructions to the sitter even as she is practically dragged out the door.

On the way to the church party, Carrie tells her husband when to turn even though they have been to this friend's home several times. Liz is the Driver's Ed teacher in her car, reminding her husband not to follow too closely behind the truck in front of them. And Sue complains that her husband needs to drive faster because they are late.

By the time the three couples arrive at the party, they are frazzled but glad to be there. The women greet their friends enthusiastically, join right into the middle of conversations, and soon find the host to inquire how they can help. Before long they are positioning the food on the tables, planning a seating arrangement, encouraging the hostess to pick someone to pray so they can get started, and helping to organize the serving line.

During dinner, they enjoy conversations with those around them, especially others who enjoy a good debate. Their tables are never short of chatter—even if no one else has anything to say, they do. And they each seem oblivious to the fact that they often interrupt others, talk over their husbands, and answer questions directed to someone else. There is no question that these three like to have their hands in many things.

On the way home, they intersperse driving instructions to their husbands with comments about how wonderful the night was but how it could have been better organized. While calculating how much to pay the sitter, they each look ahead to the next day's activities and plan how to get everything accomplished.

Although on the outside these three women seem very similar in their view of the world and their interactions with those around them, a closer look shows something different. Let's look at each of their backgrounds and see if we can glimpse the unconscious inner core that may be motivating each of them.

*Liz*

Liz was raised in a small northeastern town. Her father abandoned her and her mom and older brother when she was six years old. She didn't see him for years after that, even though she knew that he was around somewhere because he occasionally sent money to her mom. Even though Mom worked hard and provided for their basic needs, finances were always tight. Mom was always quick to blame that on her dad, saying, "If your dad really loved you, he'd send the money he owes." Mom often talked badly about Dad: how he treated her, how he was never around when she needed him, or how he was now married to some "bimbo" (whatever that was). Liz knew that Mom was angry much of the time and never seemed to like men much. She was harder on Liz's older brother than she was on Liz. Liz remembered her mother dating a few times as the kids got older, but she never seemed to enjoy herself and always had something negative to say about the guy. She even discouraged Liz from dating and talked negatively about the boys Liz went out with in high school. Liz was never sure why her mother held this opinion of men, but her mom just kept telling her, "Watch out, guys are just out to hurt you."

Then one day Liz understood what her mother meant. It was on a date during her first year in college. She had just started seeing this guy a few weeks before, and she was really starting to like him. That evening, things got a little out of hand physically, and when Liz tried to get away, he refused to let her. As this man forced himself on her, Liz recalled her mother's words, "Watch out, guys are just out to hurt you." Why hadn't she listened? Why had she put herself in a position to be taken advantage of? Liz never told a soul what happened to her that night. She pushed it all aside and pretended it never happened. On the outside she looked happy and playful, but inside she vowed that she would never let a man control or hurt her ever again. Although she eventually continued dating and later married, she developed a wall of protection around herself that kept men at arm's length. She made her own decisions, did what she wanted to do, and basically controlled her own life (and often everyone's around her too).

*Carrie*
Carrie grew up in the Midwest. She was the oldest of four and the only girl. Both of her parents were employed and expected her to be in charge of her siblings at a fairly young age. She

loved her parents and her brothers but often felt overwhelmed by the responsibility given her. She learned that one way or another certain things just had to be done, and it was usually up to her to figure out how. She became a creative problem solver, a skilled manipulator, and a master of excuses just to survive and to do the best she could for her parents and brothers. Her parents praised her ability to control her siblings and to get things done. Even when her parents were home, they often abdicated their parenting responsibilities to her "because you're so good at handling things like this, Carrie." At first this praise made her feel important, but eventually she felt that her parents' love depended on how well she performed. They gave her approval for being in charge and in control; however, they seldom praised her in other areas. So to gain the approval she desperately needed, she learned to develop the skills that her parents valued. She got involved in organizations that let her arrange large events, she ran (and won, of course) for student body president in both high school and college, and she chose a major in college that moved her toward high-powered career positions. And all along the way, her parents and others gave their strong approval. She became tough, firm, an overachiever, and a general can-do girl. She loved how it felt and the praise it earned her.

*Sue*
Sue was born giving orders to the delivery room staff and hasn't stopped yet. She was the youngest of three daughters and the biggest challenge of them all. Her parents were never sure if that was just because of her personality or because they were so much older when they had her. They had tried for years to have another child unsuccessfully and thought they never would. Then this amazing bundle of energy came.

Her parents described her as a free thinker and "our little attorney" by the time she was three. She was always getting into things, not so much to make a mess as to figure them out. Her favorite word was *why?* and the word she refused to acknowledge was *no.*

School was a necessary evil. She and her teachers often had to agree to tolerate each other for the year. She was always telling others what to do and how to do it. She directed the playground activities. Her friends described her as "bossy." She hated team projects because no one ever worked as hard or fast as she thought they should. Once she had an idea, she struggled with why everyone else didn't think it was the best idea in the world. She was self-motivated and energetic. At times that got her in trouble. She liked to debate for the sake of debating, but it was even better when she believed in her arguments. She was passionate about life and being and doing the most she could. She had dreams and aspirations and encouraged those around her to take risks and push themselves. These traits have led her throughout her life.

**COMING UP NEXT**

After peeking into the early lives of these three women, we can gain an entirely new perspective of the motivation behind their strong wills. All are married, and their interactions with the world look similar. Although one is apt to get angry more quickly, while another struggles more with low self-esteem, some qualities remain the same. All three are very strong willed. But was that what God intended for them? Maybe—maybe not.

They need to evaluate the sources of their strong-willed personalities. What is happening inside these women is a better indicator of how much they should accept their strong wills. All three are Christians and struggle with the concept of submission. They cycle through feeling like lousy examples of Christian wives or saying, "That's just the way God made me. Deal with it!" Neither attitude is correct. Each of them needs to take time to determine where her strong will came from so she can better understand how to manage it. That's what we'll do in the next chapter.

# CHAPTER 4

# Where Personality Comes From

OUR PERSONALITY AND WAYS of interacting with our world develop from several different sources. The theories and research regarding personality development are vast and often contradictory, and this one chapter could never hope to summarize them. Still, let's simply look at a few of the more commonly acknowledged influencers of personality and how these may create a strong-willed temperament.

**WHAT TYPE OF ROCK ARE YOU?**

Personality can be likened to a rock. We are born with our basic personality or type of rock. Your type of rock may be different from those around you. One person is marble; another is granite, sandstone, or slate.[1] The differences in our basic raw material and personality can begin to be noticed even at birth. I consider this part of our personality the God-given part. This is the basic foundation of who you are, and no matter what, this raw material never changes.

We can all agree that there is a type of rock out there called *strong willed*. You may be formed out of that raw material. This personality type is easily identifiable in children. These are the babies who are born giving orders and making things happen. They are naturally inquisitive, independent thinkers, and internally driven. Much like Sue they are natural leaders and motivators.

This type of woman holds both the positive and not-so-positive traits of being strong willed throughout her life, because it's what she is made of. The positive traits work for us and don't need much of our attention. However, those not-so-positive traits can cause us difficulty in life and do need to be addressed so that we will avoid hurting others and ourselves.

Even if God made you this way, your personality may be your "thorn in the flesh" that you will have to constantly commit to Jesus (refer to 2 Corinthians 12:7). You'll need to repeatedly ask Him, not you, to be in control of it. You can't say, "I was born this way, and no one can change how they were born," and expect that to be an adequate excuse for continuing in sin. That excuse has been used by others to explain away even things like homosexuality and addictions. It just doesn't fly. Being "born that way" doesn't give you freedom to act however your natural self wants to act. You still must learn discipline, surrender, and balance to allow your strong will to be effective for God and productive, not destructive, within relationships. Don't get me wrong—I'm including myself here too.

You must learn to focus on yourself correctly and on what changes you can make to improve your relationship with your husband and stop spending your time figuring out how he needs to change. You must learn to apply your strong-willed personality in such a way that it brings glory to God and growth to you and those around you.

You can choose how your raw material looks. You can

remain very raw and untreated — or you can polish yourself up to shine and reflect the best parts of yourself. That's up to you.

## TOOLS THAT SHAPE US

So, if our basic personality is God-given and we can't change it, then why have this discussion? Why not just accept it and move on? The answer is this: Although our basic personality can't change, our shape can be altered. We need to evaluate the shape our personality takes and the things that cause our shape to change. Everything from our intellect, culture, nationality, home environment, parental expectations, economics, and much more can serve as the hammers and chisels that sculpt the rock of our personality. To understand the source of our strong wills, we need to identify these influencers. Some of these tools also might have shaped a different type of rock to look like a strong-willed one. Someone may start out with a milder personality style but life experiences have taken bits away or added walls that now make this person appear stronger willed than she really is. Let's consider a couple of these.

### Life Events and Experiences
The life experiences that can shape our personality begin as early as birth. Babies born prematurely or with serious illness have often been described as being fighters or survivors, and that determination to live may later become a determination to succeed. Many life experiences that shape strong-willed personalities are considered negative. These often occur early in life but can still shape us even if they occur later. Things like abuse and neglect; traumatic

experiences such as a natural disaster, death of a parent, rape, a significant betrayal by someone we love, or hurtful adult relationships can all foster a strong personality that is determined to protect the self "because no one else is going to."

Of the three women we discussed in chapter 3, Liz's strong-willed personality was most shaped by life experiences. Her father's desertion when she was a child and the rape in college are both traumatic experiences that play significantly into her need to be in control. She no longer trusts anyone (especially not men) to protect her and keep her safe. She has developed a wall around her heart for protection.

Have you done the same? Only you can evaluate where your heart is and why your will is so strong and difficult to control. Why is it so prominent in your relationships? If the real reason you demonstrate a strong-willed personality is for protection as a result of past experiences, then you need to understand—deep inside where it counts—that Jesus is your source of protection. You must train yourself to trust Him and stop relying only on yourself. You may also need to work on forgiving those who hurt you in the past. (More on how to do this in a minute.)

*Family Life and Environmental Learning*
Now let's look more closely at Carrie from chapter 3. Much of her strong-willed nature results from childhood learning and parental expectations. We don't know if her basic personality was strong willed or not. But we do know that her environment definitely shaped her to be strong willed. The way we are raised teaches us so much about what it means to be a woman, what it takes to gain acceptance and approval, and what skills are necessary for survival in our world.

Our parents have a huge impact on how our personality develops. Cultural values and even your nationality can play a big part here as well. (We'll look more at some of those influences in chapter 5.) Growing up with a strong-willed mother who takes control of most of the workings of the home and serves as the "man of the house," or a mom who has been hurt and now hates men and tells you so, can shape your rock in the strong-willed direction. Being left to your own devices to survive, being made responsible for younger children at a young age, or simply being praised mainly for the things you do also helps to form your strong-willed nature.

If you are demonstrating a strong-willed personality that reflects childhood learning patterns and a need to gain others' approval to feel valuable, then you need to cultivate a deep awareness that Jesus values you for who you are, not for what you do. You also need to learn to accept and approve of yourself and work to seek the approval of your heavenly Father, not that of your earthly counterparts. (More on how to go about doing this coming up.)

**SOME OF ALL THREE**

When you look into these three possible sources of your strong will—God-given temperament, family learning, and life experiences—you may realize that your strong will comes from more than one source. I believe my strong will is a result of all three sources.

I believe my strong will originated from a God-given personality style. I wasn't extreme in this as a child and didn't drive my parents nuts with incessant questions or challenges. But I did think my way was best and knew how to manipulate others to get what I wanted. My tactics may have been less obvious and offensive than some of the more openly identifiably strong-willed children. Where they might use direct defiance, I used dramatic interpretation and sweet talk to manipulate. But regardless, it was still manipulation, and I usually walked away feeling like I had won.

I always had something to say (just ask a few of my teachers), and I knew the answers to everyone's problems, or at least what I had determined their problems to be. I was never good at team projects because I couldn't understand why everyone else didn't see that my suggestions were best or didn't organize things the way I would. I became easily frustrated when people didn't work and think as fast as I did. I was told I was bossy, but they just didn't understand that I was simply helping people do what they needed to do.

Once I was explaining that I had figured out what everyone needed, and if they would just listen to me, their lives would be saved. I was eight years old and in the second grade. My family had been attending a revival all week at our church with a real hellfire-and-brimstone evangelist. By the end of the week, I was down on my knees repenting (it took that preacher all week to get through my critical thinking and analyzing to get me to make a decision). But once that decision was made, I was bold and passionate about my choice and believed everyone around me needed to get on board. That included everyone on the second-grade playground.

At recess, I set up my pulpit under the big slide and exclaimed to everyone within earshot that they needed to be saved. I preached loud and hard. I explained, just like that preacher did, that each and every one of them was going to burn in hell, and their parents too, if they didn't get on their knees and beg Jesus for forgiveness! When I noticed kids crying, I was sure I was getting through and preached all the louder. Although my future in evangelism looked bleak as I was hauled away to the principal's office, I never did grasp what was wrong with my actions.

My strong-willed nature served me well as I grew. I was strong in my convictions and stood firm against peer pressure. I was driven and self-motivated, although I often procrastinated in schoolwork and responsibilities, "because I work better under pressure." Yet I hardly ever realized the adverse effect my procrastinating could have on people around me, because I was focused on what I needed or wanted. More than once I begged my mom to stay up late to help me type a paper that was due in just a few hours. Even when I became an adult, my husband and children were repetitively subject to my irritable mood and short temper when I felt under extreme pressure to get something done after procrastinating.

Since I can demonstrate that part of my strong will is God-given, does that mean all of it is? I don't think so. Since I believe God created it in me, does that mean it is always good and positive? Of course not. As I've stated, other forces have affected the extent to which my strong will has developed over my life.

I can also point to how my family environment helped to chisel out a more defined strong will in me. I grew up watching and learning from a strong-willed mother. Her childhood experiences had created in her an inner strength and a survivor's mindset that served her well. She is a logical and critical thinker and an amazing problem solver. She has been labeled a troublemaker on more than one occasion, because she's not afraid to stand up for what she believes and knows to be right. She's willing to ruffle feathers if that's what it takes to right a wrong. I love seeing that in her, and I realize that her influence played a big part in who I am today.

Both of my parents have encouraged and praised all of their children's accomplishments and instilled a belief that we can do anything we set our minds to. My dad especially dreams big and marches to a different drum when it comes to business. He is not content with the mundane or mediocre. He is a risk taker. I've often described him as a man who's made and lost millions of dollars and then got right back up the next day to do it again. One of his favorite sayings from my childhood was, "I ain't scared of nothin'," and I believe it! His influence also helped me develop a more defined strong-willed personality and a belief that there's nothing wrong with doing things my way. Of course, that belief isn't always correct.

Now don't get me wrong. I'm not saying my family is perfect. Two strong-willed parents can be a formula for trouble. I have watched those two strong personalities collide with each other, and it usually wasn't a pretty picture. Nonetheless, their influence shaped my already existing strong will.

Overall I believe my parents were positive influences who strengthened my strong will. On the other end of the spectrum, however, negative influences also strengthened my strong will. One key experience that shaped me was being sexually abused as a child.

I was abused by a man whom my parents and I believed we should have been able to trust. But obviously we couldn't. I was scared and unsure how to handle it, and so did nothing for quite some time. That was long before parents, teachers, or society at large talked openly with children about abuse and how to deal with it. So I was on my own to figure it out. Eventually I got brave enough to tell someone in hopes of getting the abuse to stop. So I chose someone who again I thought I could trust. But I realize now as an adult that telling the wife of your abuser isn't wise. My hopes were quickly dashed and my confidence broken when a confrontation led to complete denial and disbelief of my story. I was crushed and felt more alone than before. I vowed right then that I would never risk telling another soul. The rejection and disbelief were as painful as the broken trust and abuse. I think it was that very day when a wall began to form around my heart. It was up to me to keep myself safe. I could trust no one completely. I was strong, and I would learn to be stronger if that's what it took! No one was going to hurt me like that again.

Eventually the abuse did stop, but the impact of that life experience has stayed with me. I broke my vow many years later and did tell my husband and my parents about my experience. I finally received the support and validation that I so needed as a child. But the damage had already been done, and the walls were so well developed that I hardly realized they were there. I didn't need anyone to take care of me; I was fine taking care of myself. That belief has caused difficulties in my marriage because I'm married to a man who is God-created to be a protector. When he tries to protect, I often fight him, saying things like, "I'm a big girl, and I think I can take care of myself." After many years I realize that he's not saying I'm not capable of taking care of myself. He just doesn't want me to have to. He wants to help keep me safe, and I have to learn to let him. And I had to learn to forgive the people who hurt me so deeply. It is only through reaching forgiveness that you begin to break down your wall of self-protection to allow God and others back in.

## WHAT DO I DO IF MY STRONG WILL IS NOT GOD-GIVEN?

It's important to evaluate to what degree your strong will is from God or from other less-than-holy sources. If it's mainly the former, then celebrate and learn to use your God-given personality to do mighty things for Christ and to bring Him and your husband honor. But if it's more the latter, then you need to heal from your past hurts and learn to lean only on God for strength.

So how exactly do you do that? I will talk briefly about some of the steps to resolving and healing from past issues, but I also encourage you to seek counseling from a qualified Christian therapist to help you with these issues.

*Talk About It*

First of all, you need to talk about what happened. Many people who experience a traumatic event, especially during childhood, never talk about what happened or how they felt. Choose carefully whom to talk to about these issues, but you must stop keeping secrets. Tell someone you trust or find a respected Christian counselor to share your experiences with. Breaking the silence is more helpful and empowering than you could ever imagine.

*Forgive*

Once you have had a chance to process the events with someone you trust, you can move toward forgiving those people who hurt you. This can be one of the hardest parts of letting go of the past. People often have difficulty forgiving because they believe forgiveness to be something that it is not. Let's consider what forgiveness is *not* in order to better understand what forgiveness is.

Forgiveness is *not* amnesia. Forgiving and forgetting are different acts. Actually, Scripture doesn't say that God forgets our sin. It says that God "remembers your sins no more" (Isaiah 43:25). There is a difference. God is capable of forgiving and then chooses not to remember it or bring it back up in the future. As humans, we definitely do not excel at choosing not to remember what others have done to hurt us. Once something is in our minds, especially something painful, it is difficult to completely forget it ever happened. But we can make the choice not to bring the incident back up. I once heard a woman say, when reminded of a past hurtful incident, "I distinctly remember having chosen to forget that." What a wonderful way to live. Forgiveness must be given even in the face of remembering. And actually, forgiveness enables us to begin to refocus our minds by avoiding the constant rehashing of the event.

Forgiveness is *not* acquittal. In other words, forgiveness does not mean that the person who hurt you is found blameless and without responsibility. After we recognize the individual as responsible for the hurt he or she caused, then we can reach a point of forgiveness. God forgives us after we have identified that we have done something wrong, taken responsibility for it, and asked for His forgiveness. Can you imagine going to God and saying, "I didn't really do anything wrong, but please forgive me anyway." Forgiveness also doesn't mean the slate is wiped clean. Even with forgiveness, damage must be repaired and consequences experienced.

Forgiveness is *not* approval. When we forgive, we are not telling whoever hurt us that we approve of what he or she did. Think about it: If we approved of what the person did, there would be no need for forgiveness. Many people get stuck here and think that if they forgive, they are saying it's okay. This idea seems to come from a response I hear people give children all the time. When your children do something wrong and you are teaching them to ask for forgiveness, how do you do it? If you are like many people, you teach your children to say they are sorry for whatever they did wrong. Then how do you respond? Many parents reach down to give them a hug and say, "It's okay." Maybe a better response would be, "I agree with you that what you did was wrong, and I am choosing to forgive you." Forgiveness is saying, "No, it's not okay, but I'm choosing to forgive you anyway."[2]

*Put Your Past in Perspective*
Sometimes when we are dealing with a past that is full of hurt and pain, it becomes all we can see. Your past is important but not all important. Becoming overly focused on your past would be like driving a car while staring into the rearview mirror. If you are planning to drive in reverse, I guess that might be okay. But I don't know too many people who want their life going backward. So if you want to move forward in your life, focusing on the rearview mirror could be devastating and destructive.

The other extreme—driving while ignoring the rearview mirror—could be just as dangerous. It might not be bad for a while, as long as you only go straight. No switching lanes, turning, or quick stops. But as soon as you decide to make a move, it helps to know what's behind you.

So if staring into the rearview mirror and ignoring it altogether are both unhealthy, then why is it there? The purpose of the rearview mirror is perspective. You need it to drive your car safely through the twisting highways of life. You need to check in periodically with where you have been and what may be lurking behind you. And just as driving a car is safer with a rearview mirror, maneuvering your life is also much easier and safer if you have a proper perspective on your past. Just as the rearview mirror takes up only a small part of your visual field when driving, your past should take up only a small part of your vision for your life. You should never let your past become so all encompassing that it blocks your view of what lies ahead. Also, don't ignore your past to the point that its pain and dangers can sneak up and overtake you. Your past is there to give you perspective about where you have been, not to control where you are going.

*Learn to Trust*

If your strong-willed personality came from hurtful life experiences or family influences, you likely have a mindset of self-reliance. For whatever reason, you may struggle to trust others to protect or provide for you. Or you may believe your value is based solely on what you can do for others and therefore can't accept the concept of unconditional love. Either way, you have likely developed a belief that you can't rely on anyone but yourself for love, acceptance, or protection. This can become a harmful belief system that sounds like this: "No one else will take care of me, so I will!" This belief leads to a self-centered and self-protective pattern that pushes others away, even God.

Do you struggle to trust God? To really believe that He loves you unconditionally? Or do you believe you have to perform for God to bless you? Do you trust that He wants good things for you? When you are focused on taking care of yourself, you can't let go and let God in. I know you may want to explain to me why your self-reliance and self-protection are justified. And I'm sure all your reasons are good ones, but the truth is, although you may have needed those traits in the past to help you survive, you don't need them now. Your life experiences may have been so horrible that without the ability to take care of yourself you may not have made it to today. I understand that. I also know that most likely whatever happened to you was not your fault or your responsibility. However, today you are an adult and can make healthier choices for yourself. Now it is your responsibility to make whatever changes are necessary to forgive those who have hurt you and to break down the walls that are keeping you from trusting God and loving others.

As long as a part of your strong-willed personality is a result of unresolved anger, bitterness, resentment, guilt, fear, or worry, you will not be able to glorify God with it. As long as you are using your strong will to protect yourself and refusing to forgive and heal from the past, then God can't use you to your fullest potential. God does not condone sin, and harboring bitterness and unforgiveness in your heart is sin. Only as you confess this sin and do whatever it takes to heal from the past can your God-given personality show itself. Then God can move freely within you to glorify Him in all you say and do and to truly use your strong will to draw people closer to Him.

## COMING UP NEXT

We have been talking about the many factors that can influence our strong-willed nature. One of these is our culture: what society tells us about who we should try to be. In the next chapter we will look at the fact that, regardless of what the world tries to tell us, God's design for marriage doesn't change. We will also look at cultural changes in the past hundred years that have created an atmosphere that breeds increasing numbers of strong-willed wives.

# CHAPTER 5

# Culture vs. God's Pattern for Marriage

THE MORE I'VE STUDIED God's original plan for marriage, the more aware I've become of just how far we are from what He intended. And the further away we get from God's original plan, the more uncomfortable we'll be with His instructions for how marriage is supposed to work, and the more we'll want to rework what God says in order to make ourselves more comfortable. We are so good at this that we can convince ourselves Scripture says something different than it does.

## SOCIETY VS. SCRIPTURE

Marriage began with Adam and Eve, and that's when God set forth His instructions for a successful marriage relationship. So let's start there. But let's look at it from a slightly different perspective. Instead of reading it directly from the Bible, let's read it as we *choose* to believe it. Here's the gist of the story according to the New USA Personal Standard Version:

> In the beginning, after God had created the world and everything in it, He was very pleased with all He

had accomplished. He especially enjoyed His fellowship with Adam and Eve as they walked through the garden together. He provided everything they needed and gave them only a handful of instructions:

1. This is your most important human relationship; you should leave your father and mother and cleave to each other.
2. You are to unite and become one flesh.
3. Take care of the garden and animals—have dominion over the things I have given you.
4. Don't eat from that one tree over there or you will die.

Adam and Eve lived happily in the wonderful home God had supplied for them. They enjoyed each other's company, worked together to get the chores done, and fellowshipped with God daily.

One day Eve was taking a stroll through the garden, checking on the animals, when she came face-to-face with Society. She had never noticed Society before, because she was so wrapped up in her relationships with Adam and God. She was comfortable with who she was. She was content to fulfill the role God had given her and to be the wife she was created to be.

But today Society got in her face. The things he said were foreign to what she had known. He described a world that existed out there that he was a part of. She could hardly imagine the things he described. Why hadn't God told her about all these available options and freedoms?

As Society described his world, Eve's head spun

with the possibilities. The world that had been made to provide for all her needs suddenly felt small and suffocating. She was hearing of a world where she could acquire knowledge, be her own person instead of just Adam's helper, and support and take care of herself instead of everyone else. Suddenly the things that had once fulfilled and sustained her, that had given her a sense of value, now made her feel used, empty, and devalued.

Society said she was settling for being second best when there was a world out there that could make her feel like number one. He even told her she could be like God Himself.

*So, that's why God never told her about this—He didn't want the competition! All these rules that God set forth weren't really for her good, they were just to control her.*

Eve's mindset shifted. She wanted what Society offered. She wanted to be all that she could be and more. She wanted to be free to make her own decisions, to live her own life, and to set her own rules. She was tired of being second best.

*"A helpmeet? I think not! Why can't Adam be my helpmeet awhile? I've watched him do his jobs around the garden. They don't look that hard. I can do that. Actually, now that I think of it, I have been doing several of these jobs already. He just never noticed. Well now he will!"*

And with that thought, she took a great big bite of what Society offered. Then she offered it to Adam and told him to bite off some.

It wasn't long before God came for His regular

visit. But this time things were different. Adam and Eve didn't run out to meet Him. When He asked why, the excuses flew. Adam went first and bailed out by saying it wasn't his fault: "*You* made that woman, and *You* gave her to me, and *she* made me do it. If You had never made her, none of this would have happened."

It was obvious to Eve right then that it was a good thing she bit into what Society offered, because now it was apparent that this man God had put in charge was not the man for the job. He had wimped out and blamed everyone around him, including God. He had dropped the ball, and she was more than willing to pick it up and run with it. If he was not going to explain this to God, then she would. It was obviously going to be up to her to inform God what had changed and convince Him that this way was better than His way.

She explained how Society had told her about the world he was a part of and how she could become so much more than what she was. She told God she was disappointed that He hadn't shared this with her, but that wasn't the important thing. What was important now was that God understand her need to make some changes in His original plan. She explained how His rules limited her from being and doing all she could. She made sure He understood how these changes would also benefit Him, because after all, as she grew in knowledge and power, she'd be better equipped to help Him out whenever He needed it. Since it was obvious from this interaction that the man God had put in charge was not a take-charge kind of guy, the best man for this job was a woman.

In the short amount of time that Eve had been

feasting in Society's world, she had acquired much knowledge. She now had strong verbal skills, and her arguments were clear and convincing. Her presentation was so elegant, enthusiastic, and thought provoking that God was soon convinced that she had a point.

Later that day, God sat down with Adam and Eve and let them off the hook for setting so many rules for them. He explained that His intention had not been to control either of them, but now He understood how they felt. He was willing to discuss how things might change in order to better fit with what Society had taught them. They spent the afternoon rewriting the rules to make Adam and Eve more comfortable. And they lived happily ever after, or until one of them decided this marriage was restricting them from being all they could be and wanted out. Then it was easy to just divorce and move on, because Society had told them this was okay too.

## GOD'S PLAN NEVER CHANGES

I know that was extreme and somewhat sarcastic. But I was hoping to make an important point. What do you think? Is this how Scripture plays out in your mind? I know many of us want to say, "No way!" But, if we're honest, isn't that what we're doing every time we say, "Submission is outdated" or "That's not what God meant"? We're trying to say God didn't know what He was doing when He laid out the original plan for marriage—that He didn't think about how society would be thousands of years later. Or that He wasn't referring to strong-willed wives when He wrote the Bible.

When sin entered the world, things did have to change.

God had to provide a way to restore our relationship with Him. But the blueprint for marriage did not change. God knew from the beginning that sin would enter the world and that relationships would be affected. Being all knowing as He is, He made the original blueprints with everything necessary to sustain a relationship within a sinful world. He placed order among what He knew would create confusion. And as long as the order He established is maintained, relationships can be healthy and fulfilling. People within these relationships can be all that He intended them to be. We reach our fullest potential within His plan, not outside it.

God did not tell Adam and Eve, "Okay, since you want to do things your way, I guess I'll adjust my plans. Let's work together on some new rules that will make the two of you more comfortable." And the same goes for us today. God is not adjusting His blueprint for marriage to make us more comfortable. The rules and responsibilities of relationships are the same today as they have always been. The blueprint does not change just because you . . .

have been married seven or more years,
  have three children,
    experienced bankruptcy,
      got your feelings hurt,
        were abused as a child,
          missed a job promotion,
            got married because you "had" to,
              are living beyond your means,
                married a "loser" or a "control freak,"
                  or even because you are a strong-
                    willed wife.

The original plan has never changed for any reason and never will. We are not here to convince God to change His plan. We are here to obey His commands. That is the only way we can see our marriages heal—then society will understand that God's way is the only way to have a healthy, sustaining marriage. Obedience is the only way we as strong-willed wives will experience the fullness of God's plans for us and our marriages.

## IF GOD'S NOT GOING TO CHANGE, WHO IS?

God's plan for marriage is revealed throughout Scripture. He didn't tell us to leave our father and mother and cleave to our spouse without telling us what that means or how to do it. The problem is not that the instructions are not available but rather that we either don't read them or don't like what we read. Therefore, it is our fault, not God's, that our marriages are faltering or breaking down. Are we praying for God to restore our marriages and the marriages of the world? Of course we are. But the real question is, how are we praying? If you're anything like me, you may be praying something like this:

"God, please help Jim understand how he's hurting me. Show him through Your Holy Spirit where he needs to be more like Christ, demonstrating his love for me 'just as Christ loved the church.' Please restore our relationship to the place You intended it to be. In Jesus' name, amen."

Doesn't that sound holy and spiritual? Not bad, if I do say so myself. I have interceded on behalf of my husband. God and I should have Jim whipped into shape in no time.

But God is not interested in how I can help Him change Jim. He is, however, very interested in the status of my marriage. And when things are faltering, He wants to help. But as long as my prayer is primarily on fixing Jim, we won't get very far. To be honest, most of the time the problem isn't with Jim, it's with me. My strong-willed nature wants my way, tries to prove I'm right, refuses to let him protect me, or tries to tell him how to do his job. So the problem originates with me. And that means it won't go away until I open myself to God's truth and am willing to see myself as God sees me.

When I don't obey the commands God set forth for marriage, such as submitting to and respecting my husband, then I'm living in sin. It's as simple as that. Disobedience is sin, and sin is disgusting to God. So can you imagine how disgusting my life must look to God while I'm trying to act spiritual and pray for my husband?

Let's take this a step further. If I am living in a state of rebellion and sin, Scripture says He can't hear my prayers. Isaiah prophesied, "Your iniquities have separated you from your God; your sins have hidden his face from you, so that he will not hear" (Isaiah 59:2). And John wrote, "We know that God does not listen to sinners. He listens to the godly man who does his will" (John 9:31).

So not only does my sin disgust God, but now He's also unable to hear this wonderful prayer I'm lifting up to Him on behalf of my ever-so-needy husband. Great! Now I'm stinky and dirty *and* wasting my time. Maybe my time would be better spent taking a Holy Spirit bath. The real change will occur when I decide to review the commands God has given *me*, confess *my* sin of disobedience, and ask Him to help *me* make the changes I must make in order for Him to restore the marriage to where He intended it to be.

We know this is the right thing to do. But putting it into practice is much harder than we likely expect. Noticing what others are doing wrong is so much easier and more comfortable than looking at our own sin. Our selfish nature and personal pride are two of the biggest roadblocks we'll have to overcome if we are to reach our God-given potential. As we work to make these changes, think about this statement I heard once in a sermon: "God doesn't change His law to match our hearts. But He can change our hearts to match His law."

## YOU'VE COME A LONG WAY, BABY—MAYBE TOO FAR

In order to face what we are telling ourselves, we need to look at what our society is whispering (or maybe yelling) in our ears. I've suggested that society played a huge part in getting my updated Eve to change how she looked at marriage. Although we can't altogether avoid the messages that society sends, we can make sure we are aware of them and how they do or don't line up with God's design.

Why are there more strong-willed wives today than ever before? This book simply never would have been written fifty or sixty years ago. I believe it has to do in large part with the significant changes our culture has undergone in the past hundred years. Several of these changes have paved the way for an increase in strong-willed wives and for this personality style to become more and more accepted and even encouraged. Let's take a look.

Life in the 1800s and early 1900s was in a totally different world. Although life was very difficult then, in many ways it was simple. The majority of the country's population lived in rural areas, working hard just to survive. The whole family was active and helping as they grew their own food, made their own clothes, and built their own homes. There was little focus on keeping up with the Joneses because the Joneses were doing the exact same thing they were: trying to survive. There was no room for individual goals, careers, or directions. Togetherness was essential to the survival of the family. Separateness meant disaster and possibly death.[1]

I'm not suggesting that there were no strong-willed wives in the pioneer days. I'm sure there were. But these women were strong in more than just personality, and their strength helped keep the family together and afloat. They were family focused, not self-focused. And they used their strength to grow their entire family to a better place.

Today it's a different story. With the advancement of technology, many jobs can be done easier and faster. The majority of our population has moved into urban settings, and within America our focus has turned more to what we can acquire than what we can produce. And although our world may not be as physically hard to manage, it has taken on a level of complexity that can easily overwhelm us.

*Selfishness*

We constantly compare ourselves to what others have, because we see it every day through TV commercials, billboards, and our neighbor driving up in a new Lexus. We feel deprived if we don't have it all, and we are more focused on self than anything else. Dennis Rainey has said of our culture, "Today selfishness is eroding the cement of commitment—causing marriages to crumble."[2] We are a society that breeds separateness and selfishness.

*The Feminist Movement*

Strong-willed wives now not only have the time and energy to reach out for their own goals and careers, they are encouraged to have them and to meet them. Since the 1960s when the women's movement took flight, society has told women that they really aren't women unless they stand up and prove it. They aren't reaching their full potential unless they leave the home and do something for themselves. They're just the same as men and need to act as such. They need to stand up and take over. And many have.

James Dobson, PhD, describes the events of the 1960s this way:

> This era brought a new way of thinking and behaving that is still with us today. Never has a civilization so quickly jettisoned its dominant value system, yet that is what occurred within a single decade. Not only did traditional moral standards and beliefs begin to crumble, but the ancient code governing how men and women related to each other was turned upside down. It precipitated a war between the sexes that is still being waged these many years later. . . .
>
> Everything that had been associated with maleness was subjected to scorn. Men who clung to traditional roles and conservative attitudes were said to be too "macho." If they foolishly tried to open doors for ladies or gave them their seats on subways, as their fathers had done, they were called "male chauvinist pigs."

Although these early feminists called attention to some valid concerns that needed to be addressed, such as equal pay for equal work and discriminations in the workplace, they went far beyond legitimate grievances and began to rip and tear at the fabric of the family. By the time the storm had blown itself out, the institution of marriage had been shaken to its foundation, and masculinity itself was thrown back on its heels. It has never fully recovered.[3]

The feminist movement also tried to influence how women raised their sons and daughters. It wasn't enough just to influence the current generation. Feminists wanted to influence the next several as well. Feminist writers and speakers proposed that men and women were essentially identical except for reproductive purposes and should be raised as such. Gloria Steinem, one of the most influential of these women, said, "We've had a lot of people in this country who have had the courage to raise their daughters more like their sons. Which is great because it means they're more equal. . . . But there are many fewer people who have had the courage to raise their sons more like daughters. And that's what needs to be done."[4]

When you read quotes like these, do you have any question as to why men today struggle to know what their role is or who they are? Do you wonder why our husbands may have difficulty knowing how to lead or if it's okay to lead? Do you wonder why there are so many more strong-willed wives in our generation than before? I don't.

*The Sexual Revolution*
But the transformation we see in our culture is not simply a byproduct of the feminist movement. Many other changes took place at the same time that the women's movement was gaining strength, and many of these "revolutions" were promoted, legislated, and developed by men as well as women.

The social revolution of the 1960s and 1970s was just as much about the sexual revolution as about the feminist movement. The scientific, medical, and industrial advances of that time brought about the creation of newer and more effective birth-control methods, such as the pill and latex condoms. Antibiotics and other medicines helped cure many sexually transmitted diseases and made abortions safer and thus more obtainable.

State and national governments passed laws during this period that made contraceptives available not only to married women but also to single women. And it wasn't just women pressing lawmakers to make birth control more accessible. Many men who were by no means feminists wanted sex outside marriage to be more accepted and free of consequences or commitment. Many states passed no-fault divorce laws. Although these laws did allow women to more easily escape abusive or alcoholic husbands, they also benefited men who wanted younger wives. As the sexual revolution grew, more and more men sought freedom from the confines of monogamy to experience the "free love" society was offering. Between the easy divorce and safe-sex movements, Peter Pan men were now allowed the freedom to never grow up.

It is my opinion that the increase in broken homes in the past fifty years is in large part a direct result of these societal changes. The sexual revolution, including the availability of contraception to unmarried adults, especially worked to separate sex from marriage. The development of "assisted reproduction" has now also separated childbearing from marriage. As David Gushee points out, "Assisted reproduction makes conceiving children possible for any person or combination of persons willing to pay for it: two men, two women, an unmarried couple, a single woman or man. Or two men and one woman. And so on."[5] Marriage is no longer necessary, and no-fault divorce has made it disposable. Research reveals the overwhelming impact on our culture and our families as divorce has increased. Here's just a sampling of the changes since men have abdicated their family responsibilities, women have attempted to take over, and both are accepting divorce as a viable alternative to working it out:

- The nuclear family dropped to an all-time low of less than 25 percent of all households in the 2000 U.S. Census.
- There has been an increase in juvenile delinquency and rebellion.
- There has been an increase in open homosexuality.
- One in six homes was financially supported by a woman in 1990, and that number is growing every year.
- Unmarried partners living in the same household has increased by more than 70 percent in the 1990s alone.
- The number of single-mother homes continues to increase each year.
- Thirty-three percent of babies are born to unmarried mothers, as compared to only 3.8 percent recorded in 1940.

- Of mothers with preschoolers, 62 percent were employed outside the home, as compared to only 12 percent in 1950.[6]

Maybe God's plan really did work better! He never planned for women to be in charge in our homes. He knew what He was doing when He laid down His instructions for marriage and family. We say we know better, but the proof is in the statistics. Regardless of what society tells us to do, we need to realize it's just not working. We need to be strong willed enough to fight back, go against the grain of our culture's messages, and get back to what God designed for our marriages and homes.

**COMING UP NEXT**

Understanding how society, life events, and family learning affect our strong wills is important. But if we aren't careful, this understanding could just give us more ammunition to defend our strong-willed personalities. It would be easy to stop here and accept the wonderful traits we have inside us. However, that would not help us become more Christlike.

Focusing only on the positive and not addressing how these positives can turn negative, keeps our heads buried in the sand. Avoiding the difficult aspects of our personality and their effects on our relationships won't help us learn to honor God and our husband. So next we will look at the dark side of a strong will. Through acknowledging that this side exists in us, we can learn to give it all over to God.

# CHAPTER 6

# How Positive Traits Can Turn Negative

JOANN WAS KNOWN AS a superwoman. At any moment she had her hands in eight or ten different projects, hobbies, or events. She never said no to anyone or anything and seemed to have an endless supply of energy. She was always taking on new challenges. There seemed to be nothing this mother of four couldn't do. When the bathroom shower started leaking and rotting the floor, she ripped out the whole thing, fixed the plumbing problem, and replaced the tile. When the chairman of the school carnival got sick and couldn't continue, Joann jumped in, took over, and created the best carnival the school had ever seen. She later decided on a whim that she would go back to college part-time to finish her degree. She was a jack of all trades mainly because she believed there was nothing she couldn't do. Her list of accomplishments could fill a book and did fill her life.

Her husband, Mike, was friendly and fun loving. He seemed content in just about any situation, easygoing and flexible. Although he was successful in business and had risen to the top of his company, he deferred most decisions at home to Joann because she always seemed to have every-thing under control. He often came home to find that Joann had taken on some new project, volunteered them both for a new church committee, or offered to spend the weekend helping friends move. He never knew what he was coming home to and learned not to make any personal or family plans or decisions unless he checked with her.

Most of the time their relationship worked smoothly, yet they both knew the main reason for this was that Mike was willing to step back and let Joann do whatever she set her mind to do. Just as Joann never told anyone else no, Mike never told Joann no. He said, "I gave up years ago trying to talk her out of anything. It's easier to let her do her thing. Everybody's happier that way." But were they really? Was this best for them, or was it just what they had become accustomed to?

When Joann's family relationships are evaluated at a deeper level, a different picture emerges. Joann's constant running here and there and doing more than should be humanly possible took a toll on her and the whole family. Contrary to appearances, she didn't have an eternal fountain of energy, and when she ran empty her mood changed. At home she was quick tempered, impatient, and loud. When she wanted something done, she wanted it yesterday, if not sooner. She held high standards for everyone in the family and could jump from encouraging to pushy. The emotional environment around the house centered on what type of day she'd had. If things were going well, everyone had a great time. But if the stress of outside commitments was wearing her down, then everyone had better run for cover.

She and her preteen daughter, Erika, clashed the most. Erika felt her mom had to have her nose in everything and was always trying to control her. Joann had to approve what she wore and criticized how she did her hair. But the most frustrating part of their relationship was that Mom was never wrong. After they had a yelling match and both said things that were unnecessary and mean, Erika apologized to her mom for how she had acted. But Joann never apologized.

That same trait was evident in Joann's relationship with Mike. But for Mike that was not the most difficult aspect in their marriage. He struggled most with feeling like all his friends and neighbors must view him as a big wimp or a lazy good-for-nothing. They all knew Joann was repairing plumbing, laying tile, mowing the yard, pulling out shrubs, and painting the house. How else could they see him? He alone knew he wanted to help her more and do some things himself, but Joann wouldn't hear of it. He wanted to use his abilities to take care of his family and make choices for the good of his wife and children. "I don't need your help, and I definitely don't need you telling me what to do," she said when he tried to do things he felt should be his responsibility. If he pushed the issue, the fight was on, and she didn't fight fair. She became sharp, argumentative, and downright abrasive. Although he hated how this made him feel as a husband and a father, and he hated how it made him look to others, it was easier not to fight and let her do her thing.

## TOO MUCH OF A GOOD THING

Joann was a very strong-willed wife. She had many of the positive traits that we discussed in chapter 2. However, these traits were turning negative when it came to her relationship with her family. She gave the best of herself to the rest of the world and saved the leftovers for those who loved her most. How many of us are doing the same thing? Are we letting the positive aspects of our strong will get out of control to the point that people we love are getting our second best—or worse, hurt? Do you know which of your traits turn negative? Too much of a good thing can turn sour.

In chapter 2, I emphasized that being a strong-willed wife is not something to be ashamed of. We have so many positive traits that need to be nurtured so we can do mighty things for God's kingdom. However, any one of these traits, when not brought under the subjection of our Lord and Savior, can become destructive. Being a Spirit-controlled strong-willed woman is a fine balancing act that can be accomplished only through a total surrender to Jesus.

When any of our positive traits swings out of balance, the result is almost always painful to those around us. We seldom feel the initial effects of getting off track. Those closest to us notice the effects first. Only when we see their pain do we realize that we are running in the wrong direction—again. And then our pain begins.

## PROVERBS 31 OUT OF CONTROL

To see how the positive can become negative, let's look at the Proverbs 31 woman. Most of us have read about her, and many women are overwhelmed by the thought of her. But when we read the story of this strong-willed wife, we are motivated. She's our kind of woman. She characterizes the way we see ourselves. And when we are totally surrendered to God, this is who we can be (or at least close to it). Perhaps only a strong-willed wife would identify strongly with the Proverbs 31 woman. Only a strong-willed wife could undertake such a feat as that chapter describes. But we are more than happy to step up to the challenge. The problem is not our willingness to step up but rather our spiritual state as we do so.

Every one of our positive traits is only one step away from becoming negative. If at any point we lose track of the most important verse in this chapter, then everything can turn sour. Which verse is the most important? Verse 30: "A woman who fears the LORD is to be praised." As soon as the Lord is not our center of attention and we are not constantly bringing our strong will under His direct subjection, then we are off track, and those around us had better run for cover.

What happens to the positive traits of the Proverbs 31 woman when she forgets about verse 30? Here's my rendition of this chapter if she doesn't fear the Lord:

A nagging and strong-willed wife who can find?
She is worthless to her husband, and he has total
  confidence
    in her ability to do what pleases herself.
She doesn't value him and needs him not.
She brings him strife all the days of her life.
She focuses on her ability to be productive in society
    and on having the best the world has to offer.
She is selfish in her desires.
She works nonstop from morning to dark,
    yet never feels she has accomplished enough.
She does everything herself,
    because no one can do it as well as she can.
She badgers a farmer into selling her his field,
    then decides without her husband's input to
      make it a vineyard.
She sets about her work vigorously
    and with a stubborn determination does not stop
    until she gets what she wants.
She sees that her trading is profitable

and rubs it in her husband's face, saying,
"See, I told you I was right!"
She tries to discredit her husband at the city gates
in hopes of replacing him among the elders
and proving she could do everything better.
She manipulates the merchants by giving them
things they like,
then laughs at how easily she gets her way.
She argues with all around her,
and criticism is always on her tongue.
She controls the affairs of her household,
and holds all of them to her unrealistic
expectations.
Her children rise up and call her B _ _ _ _ y,
and her husband also.
Many women do unpleasant things,
but this strong-willed woman surpasses them all.
Charm is deceptive and beauty is fleeting,
but a little of either would do her a world of good.
Give her the reward she has earned:
a lonely life full of superficial relationships
and damaged souls strewn behind her.

Now if that doesn't sting, I don't know what will.

I just presented an extreme. Just as no godly woman can accomplish all the Proverbs 31 wife does, I know that no strong-willed wife would ever exhibit all of the traits I have just described (at least not in one day). But my guess is that any of us could find ourselves somewhere among those descriptive words on most days.

Where did you find yourself? Were you there with the naggers, the overly independent, or the workaholics? Maybe you fell more in line with the stubborn, selfish, or manipulating? I know it's not a pretty picture, but if we refuse to look at what can go wrong when we are not completely surrendered to Christ, then we are more likely to fall into that pit. Learning how destructive our strong will can become will help us avoid going there and, therefore, help us avoid causing pain to those we hurt.

Let's look at some of the specific traits that can turn destructive.

## "MOTIVATING" TURNS TO "PUSHY"

When our natural tendency to motivate and encourage others is driven by either unrealistic expectations or our personal agendas, we can become pushy. When the goals we set for ourselves and others are realistic, our gentle nudges will likely be seen as encouragement. However, if the goals are unrealistic (such as expecting straight As from a primarily B-C student or expecting a nonathletic child to be the best basketball player on the court), then our prodding will likely only result in discouragement. If we don't realize our expectations are unrealistic, we can do real damage as we push even harder to get the best out of our family.

As we seek to motivate our husband and kids to try new things, take risks, or reach for the stars, they may see us as badgering them into being someone they are not. We are not here to make clones of ourselves. Work to be aware of your husband's and kids' personality styles, interests, and needs, and use your motivational skills to move them in the direction that works for them. Anything else will make them feel like they aren't measuring up to your high expectations.

## "PROBLEM SOLVER" TURNS TO "BUSYBODY"

Although we are good at solving problems, that doesn't mean we were placed on this earth to solve everyone's problems—not even everyone who lives under our roof. Other people need to solve their own problems. Others at least prefer that we wait until they have asked for our help before we just jump in and start working our magic.

Because we think fast and are capable of seeing the big picture, we tend to make quick decisions that we are determined are the absolute best for all involved. The problem is, we jump in where we haven't been asked to help and we don't always see others' perspectives. We can walk into just about any social or business gathering and see how things could run smoother. There's nothing wrong in that. However, when that evaluation turns to action without invitation, it will likely irritate the other people involved.

Not all your good ideas need to be implemented in order for the world to continue spinning. Your desire to fix problems and organize the world can cause you to step hard on some toes of those who have not asked for your help. Some things really are better off left alone. This is especially true if you are raising teenagers. These young men and women need to spread their wings and make their own decisions. They need to know that you are there for counsel when they need it and ask for it, but they also need to know that you trust them to be responsible for making good choices and solving their own problems.

## "OPINIONATED" TURNS TO "ARGUMENTATIVE"

Strong-willed wives think a lot. (Sometimes too much!) We have opinions and suggestions on just about any topic you can lay before us. We have strong passions, beliefs, and values that we hold to with an iron claw. We have no intention of letting them go, even if later we learn that we shouldn't have them. Once our mind is made up, it's extremely difficult to change, regardless of the evidence. These strong opinions can get us in trouble in a couple of ways.

Because our opinions often become set in stone, when someone challenges us, we can quickly move from gentle discussion to heated argument. With our husband, this tendency can make open and honest communication very difficult. As soon as he says something that we either don't like hearing, don't agree with, or feel we need to correct, we are off and running down a rabbit trail that will detour us as far as possible from the original topic. But we won't mind as long as we get to make our point. And we won't back down, even when we know we should, until he agrees that we were right in the first place.

I've heard it asked, "Is it more important to be right or to be happy?" As strong-willed wives, we have decided that being right is better than just about anything else in the world, including happiness. And we are willing to fight to be right for as long as it takes to prove that we are. The problem is that over time, most of our husbands have decided that nothing is worth the fight, and they will acquiesce to us just to stop the conflict. That leaves us believing we have won and only fuels our self-confidence. Our belief that we are right grows even stronger for the next go-around.

Another way this opinionated trait causes difficulties is that we can develop a closed mind. When the topic under discussion is something we hold strong opinions about, we find it hard to see anyone else's point of view. By necessity, developing strong intimate relationships involves listening to and validating others in their thoughts and ideas. This can be very difficult for us because we see a right way and a wrong way—and the right way is our way. That doesn't leave room for sharing and intimacy to occur between two people who are uniquely created and therefore different.

## "INDEPENDENT" TURNS TO "OVERLY SELF-RELIANT"

Most of us strong-willed wives like our independence. We feel strong when we can do things ourselves and take care of ourselves. We feel a sense of accomplishment when we tackle something on our own and succeed. And in most of our relationships and endeavors, this is a valuable trait. But it can go too far.

When independence is taken to an extreme it becomes overreliance on self. We convince ourselves that we don't need anyone, because we can handle everything just fine ourselves. We trust our own decisions and are confident in our ability to manage our life. The problem comes when we become so confident in ourselves that we push others away, including our husband and even God. We end up exhausted by doing everything ourselves. We don't trust others and therefore don't delegate to them. Or, if we do, we spend almost as much time checking up on them or nagging them as we would have taken to do it ourselves. We don't allow our husband to help us or fight any of our battles, because we don't want to look needy. Yet this robs him of something he needs most. When he can use his God-given abilities to provide for and protect his wife and kids, he feels masculine, needed, and important.

At least part of this overreliance on self is a result of past hurts that have taught us not to trust other people. We have grown to believe that to be safe, we have to provide for ourselves. This learned behavior causes us to build a wall around ourselves that even people close to us can't break through. At the extreme, we struggle to trust even God. We may pray for what we need but our prayers sound more like instructions to God as to how He should go about answering that prayer. Or we may pray for God's guidance but never wait for the answer, because we have already figured out the next step or we don't really expect Him to answer. We need to learn that without trust, there is no relationship with God or our husband.

## "EXTROVERTED" TURNS TO "ABRASIVE"

Our zeal can drive us past extroversion and straight into abrasiveness. We like to be the center of attention but often don't realize what we do to gain attention. We often dominate a conversation or use a voice several volume notches above the rest of the room. We are excited about what we have to say and expect that everyone else is as well. We are usually oblivious when we talk right over someone else. We don't think twice about interrupting or changing the topic mid-sentence if something more interesting comes to our mind. We justify rudeness in the name of excitement. We come on way too strong and don't realize it.

If you can imagine how annoying this can be in a social situation, just think about how frustrating it is in a marital conversation. If you are passionate about what you are discussing with your husband, you are likely a terrible listener. You determine that what you have to say is so important that it has to be said right now. As you inter-rupt and talk over your husband, who is trying to share his thoughts and feelings, you send the message that what he has to say isn't as important as what you want to say. The long-term effect of this style of communicating is a husband who shuts down and becomes quiet.

## "LEADER" TURNS TO "LONER"

In our deep desire to make a difference in our world we may reach a point of alienating those around us. Although people need a leader, they don't like to be controlled. The problem is that we strong-willed wives usually don't know how to lead without controlling. We tend to believe that everything will work out as long as we are in charge and things are being done "my way" and "now!" This perspective makes us more of a dictator than the leader we desire to be or even a member of the marital team, and people withdraw from us. Control and intimacy are opposites, and as long as we seek to control others, we end up with lots of superficial relationships but no intimacy.

You may say you like being a loner—that you don't fit in anyway. Or you decide that's the price of being in charge, so it's worth it. But if you look inside yourself, my guess is you are not as content with being the Lone Ranger as you let on. We are social creatures, and most of us like to have friends. It's only when we don't have friends that we say we don't want them anyway. But most of us truly want them. Do we want them bad enough to relinquish some control?

Are you willing to stop bulldozing over everyone and everything to get things done your way? If you want a deeper relationship with your husband—one that goes beyond the parent-child style of interaction that you likely demonstrate at least sometimes—then bulldozing has to stop and true teamwork has to begin. To get that deep intimacy, you will have to give up the need to control your husband. (More on this in chapter 15.)

## "DETERMINED" TURNS TO "STUBBORN"

Strong-willed wives know what we want and how to get it. When we set goals, we don't waiver. When obstacles cross our path, we see them as just another challenge and face them head on. We are driven and don't give up easily—it's a matter of principle to prove we can do whatever we are attempting. Pressure is more likely to make us extra productive than to make us give up.

I've always said I work best under pressure. In college I procrastinated on papers until the ninth hour, and then I'd kick it into high gear and produce a paper worthy of an A (at least in my opinion). I'm still like this. At this very minute I'm under a tight deadline to get this book finished. To me that's more a challenge than a deterrent.

But this healthy determination can become plain stubbornness. We often don't look at, or even care, what the cost may be, either monetarily or to our relationships. We can decide on something, set our mind to it, and start the process before even mentioning it to our husband.

So what happens if, when he finds out about your most recent project, he doesn't agree with it? Do you talk it over and consider backing down or delaying it? Probably not. If you're like me, you dig your heels in and brace for the fight. You have already set your goal, and *retreat* is not in your vocabulary. You can become an immovable force and will use all your skills of verbal overkill and domination to get your way. Forget submission; this isn't even cooperation.

## "FOCUSED" TURNS TO "SELFISH"

Finally, along with our determination, we are also able to shut out distractions and focus our mind on what needs to be done. But we can become so involved in what we deem important that we have tunnel vision. When we have a project, a deadline, or just a conversation that we want to engage in, we can shut out the rest of the world.

This ability to focus on what we are interested in can make us self-absorbed. When what we are doing becomes more important than what other people need us to do, there is no other word for it except *selfish*. We may demand that others do whatever else needs to be done because we're "too busy." We may then expect more of our husbands and children than is realistic. As we absorb ourselves in whatever seems interesting, who will do the necessary things we did before we became so focused? Who will do the cooking, laundry, yard care, or carpooling? Our husbands and kids likely feel neglected.

## FINAL THOUGHTS

We strong-willed wives have many wonderful traits that God has placed inside of us to bring Him glory. However, it's up to us how we use those traits. In chapter 2 we noted that fire is a good thing as long as it's controlled. This chapter has described what happens to us and our relationships when the fire within us gets out of control. A small campfire that warms campers and cooks their food can become a blaze raging out of control and destroying everything in its path. Much like that fire, our strong-willed nature, when under the Holy Spirit's control, can fulfill our God-given potential and draw us and those around us closer to Him. However, that fire within us can rage out of control and destroy whatever's in our path, including our witness for Christ.

It is up to us to be aware when our personality traits get off balance. We need to pay attention, seek balance, and always ask for God's help in keeping our personality in check.

**COMING UP NEXT**

Somewhere along the way, we strong-willed women decided we wanted to get married. What type of man did we look for? And what was he attracted to in us? With all our positive and negative traits, could he look past our negative traits and see a woman he could love forever? We could only hope.

In the next chapter we will look at these issues. We will discuss what traits strong-willed women are attracted to in a man. We will also look at the types of men who are attracted to us and why. And then we will discuss why this couple, who seemed so perfect for each other in the beginning, does not simply live happily ever after. What causes these initially positive traits to turn into something that damages our marriages?

# CHAPTER 7

# The Strong-Willed Woman
# Chooses a Man

BECAUSE WE ARE AS unique as our fingerprints, the men we date, fall in love with, and eventually marry must be just as varied. The strength of our personality traits, as well as the reasons we are the way we are, all play into the type of man we are attracted to. For those of us who attribute much of our strong will to God-given traits and/or learned behaviors from a strong mother, we will most likely choose a man who shows confidence and represents security. We look for a man who respects women and believes they are equal partners working on the same team. We want him to be a strong leader but not overbearing—a man we can trust to give us the autonomy we seek and yet still be there for us when we need him emotionally. We want him to be independent and goal driven, yet not selfish or inflexible. We want him to hold intelligent conversations and openly share his thoughts and opinions with us. We are even interested in his being open to debating topics of interest with us. We are searching for our equal.

On the other hand, those of us who are strong willed more because of painful life circumstances look for slightly different things in men. Traumatic events such as abuse or abandonment in childhood and hurtful or abusive relationships as a young adult draw us to men with a different set of characteristics. Past hurts or overcompensating for low self-esteem will likely move you to seek a man whom you believe you can trust—someone who is gentler and less openly challenging. You will most likely prefer a man who allows you to make the majority of the decisions not just because you are good at it, but because you find your security in knowing that you are in charge. You are attracted to a man who is easygoing, flexible, and slow to anger. His quiet strength and emotional stability are assets to you, as are his agreeable disposition and his desire to avoid conflict.

## THE MEN WE SEEK

Because many of us have received our strong wills from a combination of sources, we seek many different possible combinations of traits in a husband. However, a few basic traits appeal to us, whether the man has a strong personality or is more passive. Let's look at some of these.

*1. A spiritual, Christ-centered man:* Just about every strong-willed Christian wife I know says that if she was a believer at the time, the main thing she sought in her future husband was a desire to serve Christ. We want someone who can match our level of passion for our Savior. Someone who is willing to be open about his faith and who enjoys discussing spiritual topics with us. We at least voice that we want him to be the spiritual leader of our home, yet we may struggle with what we believe that looks like in real life.

*2. An encourager and supporter:* Because we're always on

the lookout for something new to keep boredom at bay, we desire a man who encourages us in these ventures. We want someone who will support our dreams and cheer us on as we face new challenges. Someone who believes with us that we can do anything and is willing to let us try. Someone who will help us be all that we can be and not discourage us from continually reaching higher.

3. *Someone who gives us respect:* Because he is secure and confident in himself, the man we seek doesn't have to prove anything to anyone. He is not on an ego trip and doesn't need to put anyone down to lift himself up. He is not intimidated by our strong will but actually seems to like the independence that we show. He respects who we are and what we want to do with our life. He seeks out our thoughts and opinions. He doesn't demand respect, yet because he is comfortable in his own skin, he seems to earn it. And he's just as quick to give it to others.

4. *Someone who is levelheaded:* We need a man who demonstrates a quiet strength and is patient and forgiving. This type of man is a perfect complement to our quick-tempered, emotionally labile, flighty personality style. He feels like a stable rock who can steady us in our storms. Because we know how easily we can go from one emotion to another and because we often speak and act long before we seriously consider the consequences of our actions, we need someone who can see past that side of us and realize that underneath there really are good intentions. A man who is quick to forgive and let it go is extremely attractive to us.

5. *A servant-hearted man:* Each of us is attracted to a man who is unselfish and interested in the needs of others — especially ours. Because of our tendency to become self-absorbed and self-focused, we are drawn to men who are willing to

make sacrifices for us. These men will put our needs, wishes, and desires before their own.

## STRONG-WILLED OR PASSIVE MEN?

Men who date and later marry a strong-willed woman each have their own reasons for doing so. But all of them are initially attracted to her because of the *positive* aspects of her personality. During these early stages of a relationship, the negative aspects of her strong will may not be completely evident or may be easily overlooked. The men who are attracted to strong-willed women can be divided into two groups: passive men and strong-willed men.

*Why Passive Men Are Drawn to Us*
Those men who by nature are more passive and quiet are often attracted to strong-willed women because they see in these women many of the traits they feel they lack. Opposites really do attract. A passive man is drawn to a strong woman's outgoing personality and assertive nature. He likes that she's a strong decision maker and feels a safe haven in that. He may have grown up in a home where his mother was a take-charge woman (either by nature or by circumstance), and he learned to be more passive. She may have made most of his decisions and done for him things he could have done for himself. He may look to continue that environment in his future home because it's what he's accustomed to—it's all he's ever known. He may not have developed confidence in his abilities to make his own decisions and therefore may want a wife who will continue this pattern. We often are attracted to a spouse who has traits in common with the parent whose personality is the opposite of ours. That doesn't

necessarily mean this is the healthiest choice, but it's what we are comfortable with and so may be what we choose.

Another possibility is that the more passive man may have lived in a home that required him to grow up too fast. He may have had adult responsibilities placed on him from a very early age, and, by the time he's looking for a wife, he may be ready to relax a bit. He may be tired of always taking care of everyone else. He may have decided it's his turn to finally be a kid and let someone else be in charge. When this is the case, he will be looking for a wife who can make decisions and manage many or all of the things he was forced to manage in his home as a child.

Men who have a more passive personality style are likely to say things like:

*"She completes me."* Passive men may feel gaps in their personality style that a strong-willed wife fills in. He knows that he's not a social butterfly, but he enjoys being around people. She helps him do that through her outgoing personality. He knows that on his own he's not likely to take the hard road when it comes to career decisions or financial risks, but initially her encouraging, motivating, and dreaming helps him take those leaps of faith. He has looked for his opposite to balance him. He is looking for someone who can encourage him to reach higher and do more than he believes he could do on his own.

*"She provides security."* A passive man often feels less confident in his abilities to provide adequately for his family's needs. He may not feel strong enough to be the spiritual leader of the home, the sole financial provider, the dominant parent, or the responsible spouse. Marrying a strong-willed woman gives him a power partner on which to lean. He likes that she has everything under control and can manage him,

the kids, the house, and anything else that comes his way. He gains security knowing that everything will be just fine as long as she's in charge.

*"She's a great decision maker."* When a passive man is faced with a decision, he often finds himself thinking and rethinking the facts and possible outcomes. He gets bogged down in trying to find the "right" or "best" decision to the point that it's difficult for him to make any decision at all. Because of his own difficulty in making decisions, he sees her quick thinking and decision making as a strength. He's attracted to her problem-solving abilities and the way she can see the big picture, analyze what's needed, and move forward without taking forever to do so. He's amazed at times at the confidence she shows in her decisions and how she seldom if ever, second-guesses herself.

*"She's assertive."* A passive man grapples with being able to stand up for himself. He is quick to give in, especially if it means avoiding conflict. He may later feel anger over yielding so quickly, but he really does hate to argue. He may feel that in many areas of life he gets the short end of the stick and that he allows himself to be taken advantage of. But his strong-willed wife would never allow that. He loves the fact that she's not afraid to stand up for what is right, even if it leads to a fight. She has strong convictions about what is right and wrong. She not only doesn't yield but also feels driven to address wrongs she comes across. He likes knowing that she is willing to handle everything from mistakes on credit-card statements to telemarketers. She doesn't accept her (or his) steak being cooked wrong at a restaurant or a repairman doing his job incorrectly. She will stand up and make right things for herself and her family. This captivates him.

*Why Strong-Willed Men Are Drawn to Us*
The other group of men who are attracted to a strong-willed woman's positive traits is those who are strong-willed themselves. These men hold many of the same positive traits we do. They are movers and shakers in their world. They have dreams, opinions, and aspirations and they are looking for a woman who can take the journey with them and not hold them back. A strong-willed man almost always enjoys a good debate about a variety of topics and is stimulated by challenges. The strong-willed man who chooses a strong-willed woman most likely grew up in a home where he watched his father and mother work together on projects, make decisions together, and strive to be the best they could be. His father was likely a respected man who gave just as much respect to his wife. He also likely witnessed strong discussions between his parents that started as friendly debates and moved to heated arguments, but weren't destructive to the relationship. He sees conflict as a way of showing interests, voicing opinions, and solving problems. He's attracted to a strong-willed woman because she is independent and has her own interests and activities that keep her busy. She is not clingy or overly dependent, so he has the opportunity for individual and "guy time" to continue engaging in his own interests, hobbies, and activities.

Men who themselves are somewhat strong willed are likely to say things like:

*"She keeps me in line."* A strong-willed man is aware just as we are that his will needs boundaries if it is to be maintained within healthy levels. Just as our positive traits can quickly turn negative, so can his, and having a strong accountability partner can reduce the possibility of his damaging those he loves. He is initially attracted to her boldness in calling him

on his stuff if he acts in a way that is not healthy or appropriate. He likes that she's not intimidated or easily manipu-
lated by him. That earns his respect.

*"She's responsible and productive."* A strong-willed man
is always on the go. He does a million things at once. He's
attracted to a woman who does the same. He especially likes
that she is willing and able to take care of all the things that
he doesn't want to make the time to do. He knows that when
he delegates something to her, it will be done right. He feels
secure in that, and it takes weight off his shoulders. Her
strengths of organizing, accomplishing goals, and generally
being able to do more than he can comprehend at times are
valuable traits in his book. He loves that she has aspirations
and is confident in her ability to accomplish what she sets her
mind to. Her drive to do as much as she can and to make the
most out of her life is intriguing to him. When she sets her
mind to do something, she doesn't accept failure or retreat.
She will do whatever it takes to make it happen.

*"She thinks for herself."* A strong-willed man is not looking
for a "yes woman." He isn't attracted to someone who just says
what he wants to hear. He is actually drawn toward a woman
who can challenge him to think things though and see things
from a different perspective. He likes that when he asks her
opinion on a problem she has just as many possible solutions
as he does. He enjoys brainstorming about life goals, vacation
plans, and financial decisions. He knows she will add to any
discussion. He loves that she's intelligent, opinionated, and
passionate about her beliefs. She's not easily swayed and has
a firm basis for why she believes what she does. Conversations
about such things are invigorating to him.

*"She's motivating and encouraging."* Although most
strong-willed men are internally driven, even they like to be

cheered on by people around them. Such a man is attracted to a strong-willed woman because of her natural tendency to be motivating and encouraging. She is an optimist who can see how to maneuver past the obstacles he faces and can persuade him to keep on trying. He sees her as his biggest cheerleader and on his team, and he believes he can do whatever he sets his mind to. She doesn't discourage his dreams, and as she's standing behind him, she's pushing him forward.

**WHAT CHANGES?**

Knowing what type of man we strong-willed women looked to marry and also the types of men who were attracted to us, wouldn't it make sense that if we found and married that type of man we would live happily ever after? That would be nice, but unfortunately it seldom works that way. The pattern of interactions between a husband and wife can change over time and create distance rather than closeness. As you probably noticed, the characteristics that attract us to each other are our positive traits. These traits convince us that we are the perfect match. However, as we've seen, these same traits can so easily turn negative and over time drive us crazy.

*Isabel and Mark*
Isabel and Mark met in college and married shortly after both graduated. They had big plans for their careers and their life together. They were the couple that everyone said would have it all because they knew what they wanted and didn't let anything stand in their way. They seemed to live a charmed life. They didn't have to struggle with whose career would come first, because both immediately landed great jobs in the same large city. They were both successful in their

respective positions and exceeded their income goals within their first two years of marriage.

They decided together to buy a house in the suburbs. They talked about when to have children and agreed that neither was ready yet. They loved the flexibility, spontaneity, and freedom they enjoyed with their current lifestyle. They were both spenders, and where they stood now that was no problem. Isabel tended to spend more on household décor and trips out of town to visit family and friends. Mark enjoyed his "boy toys." They never talked about their purchases beforehand, because they knew the money was there. And besides, they liked the element of surprise, and they were almost always happy about what the other had acquired. Although they knew they weren't saving for the future, they were enjoying the fruits of their hard work.

They worked hard and played hard. They both put in long hours to climb the corporate ladders, and when work was over they did their best to make the most of their playtime. They went out often, both as a couple and with friends. They engaged in long conversations about everything from politics and religion to what they would do when they won the lottery. And they each seemed to find plenty of time to participate in their individual interests.

Time passed. Now Isabel and Mark have a young son and a baby daughter. When their son was born, Isabel decided to stay home more. She and Mark had never discussed it, but she assumed that he agreed that as long as the children were little, she would not work as much and maybe not at all. When she told him she had requested that her job be transitioned to part time, he blew a gasket. "How in the world do you think we will be able to afford this house and all your stuff? Don't you think we should have talked about this before you just up and changed things?" And the fights didn't stop there. From about that moment on, they had more conflicts than quiet conversations. She did begin to work only part time, and as a result the financial pressures increased, because neither of them was willing to curb their spending habits. When either made a significant purchase, the other was quick to jump on them: "How could you buy that? You know we can't afford it!" The response was always something like, "Don't tell me what we can afford after what you bought last week." Their separate priorities had become a problem.

They not only didn't agree on how money should be spent, they also didn't agree on Mark's involvement in raising the kids and helping around the house. This lack of adjustment on both parts was becoming a problem. Their independence in decision making was causing additional tension.

*Alice and Kevin*

When Alice met Kevin, she was only seventeen but was more than ready to move out of her parents' house. She was tired of the conflict and abuse from her alcoholic father, and she saw in Kevin a gentle, loving man who would care for her. Kevin was four years older and had been on his own since completing high school. He was a hard worker and responsible with money. He paid his bills on time and always had food in the cabinets. She valued these habits, because they had not always been present in her childhood home. He was easygoing and quiet and never seemed to get angry. She even tested that a few times by picking a fight with him and yelling at him. He simply waited for her to finish and then quietly said something like, "I love you, and I'm sure we can work this out." She knew this was the man for her, and they married when she graduated from high school.

Their early years were fairly smooth, mainly because Kevin always gave in and let Alice have whatever she wanted. He really did love her and wanted to give her the world, but he knew that his income was limited and wasn't sure how this could continue. Sometimes she asked for something big that he knew they couldn't afford. But when he said, "I think we'd better wait a while on that" (which was his way of saying no), she got upset, pouted, and argued about why they really needed this item now and how they could make it work financially by moving this or that around. It didn't take long for his weak no to be swayed into a yes, and then he'd be working overtime to make it happen.

It was evident that Alice was in charge. At times she actively made the decisions about where they went, what they did, or how they spent their money. At other times her control came from her masterful way of manipulating Kevin to get him to make the decisions she wanted him to make. Either way, she took the role of the man of the house, and for at least several years, that was how they both seemed most comfortable.

Many years have passed, and now Alice and Kevin have two teenage daughters: Lisa (sixteen) and Kate (fourteen). Lisa is the ideal compliant child who works hard at school, practices her cello two hours a day, likes church, and isn't much interested in doing what kids seem to think is required to be popular. She's just like her dad. Kate, on the other hand, is more of a wild child. Her figure has developed, and she has lots of fashion sense, as well as a fun-loving, flirtatious manner. She's not interested in homework, culture, or church. She's most interested in her social standing with friends, and she spends hours on the phone or computer chatting.

Kevin and Alice have continued their pattern of inter-action. Alice makes or influences almost all the decisions. She appears to Kevin to be unaware of how much money he makes and how hard he works to keep them out of bank-ruptcy as she spends beyond their means. When he talks to her about it, he feels his concerns are never addressed. Alice justifies her spending by saying that he doesn't understand how much money it takes to run a household with two teen-age daughters. And then she quickly changes the topic to her worries about Kate's decisions in friends and how Kevin needs to get involved and help more. Kevin feels their rela-tionship is all about what Alice wants or needs and that she never takes time to consider what he wants and needs. He feels invisible most of the time, unless she needs him for something—mainly for his paycheck or to be the tough parent with their daughters.

Kevin has a stressful job and works long hours to provide for his family. He would love to come home to tranquility. But that doesn't happen. As a result of their finances, he has to put in more and more overtime just to stay afloat. But he doesn't mind because it keeps him away from the conflict. He's hardly ever home. When he is home, Alice does her best to corner him about what's going on with Kate and how she's been talking disrespectfully. But before she gets it all out, Kevin says, "Why can't I just come home and relax? Why does there always have to be so much conflict? You want to make all the decisions, so why can't you make the decision on what to do about Kate?"

Alice dives into conflict: "Well, maybe I'm tired of being the one who always makes the decisions. Maybe it's time for you to step up and do something! Your children need you and I need you to help out around here. Do you know that Kate called you a wimp last night when I told her it was up to you if she got to go to the dance next Friday? Do you even care? Maybe you are just a big wimp!" The fight escalated from there, at least on Alice's part. Kevin just sat quietly and tried to appear to be listening even though he wasn't. He was actually thinking about how he could sympathize with Kate. He wanted to let go and yell at Alice the way Kate did sometimes. He was so tired of being nagged about every little thing—always being told what to do and how to do it, and then later told how he did it wrong. He coped by working all the overtime he possibly could just to stay away from the house and the fighting.

**ARE WE CREATING OUR OWN MONSTERS?**

With each of the couples just discussed, you can see how their relationship has changed over the years. What initially attracted them to each other became thorns in their flesh. In Isabel and Mark we saw two very strong-willed individuals who knew what they wanted and were driven to attain their individual goals. They respected that each had their own interests and were independent in decision making and activities. They were attracted to those very traits. Mark loved that Isabel wasn't dependent or clingy, and Isabel appreciated that Mark gave her space to do her own thing. But over time those traits took their toll. Their independence began to feel more like separateness in almost every area of life. As life changed, Isabel needed Mark to be a family man—to be around more and help with the kids. Mark saw this change as Isabel becoming clingy and trying to control him by not letting him go out with his friends. The more she sought to get him involved with the kids, the more he pulled away to prove that he was in control of himself. Their separate priorities, goals, and desires were no longer interesting surprises, but now simply looked like selfishness to the other.

Alice and Kevin were experiencing a similar change. Alice was attracted to Kevin because of his gentle spirit and quiet nature. She loved that he worked hard to avoid conflict, because she had grown up with a father who seemed to thrive on conflict and actually created it. But now things were different. Kevin's passive style of relating looked to her like weakness and avoidance, and she was determined to get him involved.

Kevin, on the other hand, had been attracted to Alice's ability to make decisions quickly and to be secure in those decisions. However, now he was tired of being told what to do. He backed away even further to avoid conflict, and in response, Alice pursued all the more. The cycle of control was in full swing for both couples.

## THE CYCLE OF CONTROL

The cycle of control develops over time and tends to intensify and change as the relationship proceeds. The wife's strong-willed nature was not as evident when the focus was primarily on the positive aspects of that personality style. We all know what it's like to fall in love, sure that we have found our soul mate. When we are in that state, we are usually wearing rose-colored glasses and see everything as just a little better than it is. But over time the rose-colored glasses come off and we can see each other more clearly. Each personality likely becomes more prominent. Neither person may now act like who the other thought they were when they married. Their expectations for a happy marriage are challenged, and both feel disappointed and hurt.

The strong-willed wife reacts to relieve her internal pain by attempting to control her environment and her husband even more. She hopes that if she can control what's happening, then she can change it and relieve her pain. As author Nancy Groom explains,

> Her most common tactic is to try to change her
> husband into the kind of man she thinks she needs
> and believes God intended her to have. The absence
> of a wife's genuine acceptance of her husband
> (and he feels it keenly) sabotages his confidence in
> himself and in her. The unspoken rejection implied
> by her manipulation, however well-intentioned,
> undermines the very environment of trust and
> openness she needs if she is to flourish as a loved
> woman.[1]

Her attempt to change her husband will result in exactly the opposite of what she's trying to gain. It will make him feel unaccepted and inadequate. As his confidence breaks down, his innate fear of criticism and failure will grow, and then he will pull away emotionally and physically to lessen this pain.

By pulling away, he puts distance between himself and his wife. That distance triggers her innate fear of being rejected and abandoned. She will respond to her fear by grabbing hold even tighter to what she fears she's about to lose. She will pursue her husband more intensely and attempt to force him to interact and to give her what she wants and needs. This will often look like nagging, criticizing how he does something, telling him how to do it better, rethinking decisions he's made, demanding his time and attention, and generally controlling him in any way she can.

As this pattern continues, he will likely react by relinquishing more control to her as his only way to avoid the pain of criticism. One husband told me, "It's easier to let her do it herself or do what she tells me to do. At least I don't get in trouble that way." The passive husband does this to avoid conflict. To him, giving in to her seems the easiest way to keep things at home smooth.

On the other hand, the strong-willed husband will also likely relinquish control to his wife, but for different reasons. The strong-willed husband will relinquish control only in areas where it somehow benefits him and then only to a point. To him it's about getting what he wants, which may be more time for himself or the freedom to focus on his career. Relinquishing control to his strong-willed wife in areas such as household management, parenting, and even finances may allow him more of what he's seeking.

But either way, both husbands give up more and more of their God-given authority within the home just to keep the peace.

Eventually even a strong-willed wife gets tired of being in charge all the time and responds by trying to nag, manipulate, or coerce him into taking more responsibility. Eventually any husband (passive or strong willed) gets tired of being controlled and responds by separating himself from her. As she reacts by exerting more control, he relinquishes more control to her, and on and on it goes. Neither gets what they wanted—a healthy, intimate marriage. Over time, both get tired of these roles. She says she wants him to lead but won't let him, or she criticizes how he leads. He says he wants to be in charge but then won't make a decision or changes his mind as soon as he feels it's not what she wanted. Can you see how this cycle of control spins out of control? With each person in pain, they do what they know to do to relieve that pain. Since the pain comes from their fears, the solution is to relieve that fear. Unfortunately, what we know to do to relieve our fears is exactly what pushes our spouse's fear button. When his fear is tapped into, he responds in a way that pushes our buttons. The result is distance and a lack of intimacy.

Each of our personality styles intensifies, so over time our strong-willed nature grows more prominent. At the same time, we grow further and further from what God intended our marriage to look like, because we are focused on protecting self more than on cultivating oneness and Christlikeness.

## COMING UP NEXT

The cycle of control can be the downfall of our marriage. But what sets the cycle in motion in the first place? It starts when one or both partners experience pain or disappointment in the relationship. This pain often comes from unmet expectations that we take into marriage. Our expectations entering marriage are usually focused on self. What will I get out of being married? How do I expect to be treated? Will my husband or wife make me happy? In the next chapter we will look at what we have the right to expect from our spouse and what we are personally responsible for within our marriage.

# CHAPTER 8

# Rights and Responsibilities

CHRIS AND SHERRI SAT in my counseling office. Having been married only three and a half years, they were seriously contemplating divorce. As I listened, I reflected on how selfish so many people are. When I asked them what got them considering divorce so quickly, I realized these were two very strong-willed individuals.

Sherri was the first to speak. "He just makes me so unhappy. I have the right to some happiness, don't I?"

Chris was quick to counter. "Maybe we could be happy if you would stop spending all my money. I make the money; I should have the right to decide how it's spent."

"If I left it up to you, you'd spend every cent we have on the golf course. All you do is think about yourself. You're gone all the time and leave me at home alone. It would be nice to have a husband around once in a while so I'd at least feel like I'm married. Is that too much to ask?"

"Well, maybe if you'd stop talking to your sister on the phone all day and get the house cleaned up, I'd want to come home. The way it is now is awful. I shouldn't be expected to live like that."

On and on it went for several more minutes. The

blaming, the finger pointing, the excuses and justifications all got worse. It was all the other's fault that things were going so badly. They continued to throw daggers at one another, and as the competition continued, the weapons got bigger. It was all about who had the right to do what. By the time I stopped them, I wanted to tell them both, "You have the *right* to remain silent!" Anything short of silence at that point was going to cause more damage.

## HOW SELFISH CAN WE BE?

What I saw in Chris and Sherri may have been extreme, but unfortunately, it's an example of something I see in many couples. I meet couples who are angry not only with each other but also with the whole institution of marriage. All they see is how they've been hurt or slighted by their partner and how marriage is not all it's cracked up to be. As I've listened to them describe why they are so disappointed, it's clear that they walked into marriage with a totally wrong idea as to what it's about. I hear them saying things like:

"She's not meeting my needs!"

"I have the right to feel loved and respected, don't I?"

"What's wrong with me having a little fun with my friends? I work hard and pay the bills."

"It's my money. I make it so I can spend it!"

"All he ever wants is sex."

"Why can't she see things my way once in a while?"

On and on they go, focusing almost exclusively on what they're not getting that they believe they have the right to have. We are living in a self-focused society, and that cultural selfishness only intensifies a strong-willed personality. We already think our way is best and that everyone else should see things from our perspective. Combine that mindset with a society that tells us we should expect things our way, and you have a recipe for a multitude of very selfish people.

We live in a culture where we enjoy many rights and privileges. The court system is overwhelmed with cases filed because people feel their rights have been infringed. We are so focused on what we believe we, as individuals, deserve that we have lost track of what the United States was based on in the first place: "One nation under God, *indivisible . . .*" When we focus on self, the unity of the whole dissolves. We cannot be selfish and unified at the same time. As strong-willed wives, we cannot be self-focused and unified with our husbands at the same time either.

This focus on our personal "bill of rights" rather than on others' needs is destroying our marriages. When a strong will is rooted in a mindset of self-reliance, we become self-centered and self-protective. We focus on who we are individually and what we need, instead of on our husband and our marriage. Unified, healthy marriages are impossible as long as we hold more tightly to our individuality than our unity. Regardless of whether we are married to passive men who let this side of us grow or to strong-willed men who fight for their own bill of rights, our marriages will suffer.

Scripture does not validate selfish individualism in any relationship and especially not in marriage. Rather, we're told to leave our father and mother and "cleave" to one another (Genesis 2:24, KJV). We are told to join together with such closeness that we become "one." We are to blend, not separate.

So why do we have so much separateness in our marriages? I believe it has to do with our focus on our personal rights. Let's take a look at how the Bible describes our marital bill of rights and see how this affects our relationships.

## MY MARITAL BILL OF RIGHTS

In my quest to better understand what God says we have the right to within our marriages, I studied Scriptures specifically related to this topic. To my surprise, I didn't have to search long. As I studied, the list of God-given rights within marriage became clear. Here's what God says our rights are in marriage:

1.
2.
3.
4.
5.

There they are. What? You missed them? Well, so did I. Scripture does not focus on our rights within relationships. Why not? Let me explain.

A right is something I am entitled to receive or a protection I should have. It's about entitlement. If we feel entitled to something and then it doesn't happen, we feel angry and slighted. Our concept of rights keeps us focused on ourselves, protecting ourselves, and demanding for ourselves what we believe we deserve. I'm not saying there's no need for individual rights. I'm completely aware of this need in many areas. As a matter of fact, in my own profession as a clinical psychologist, we have a patient's bill of rights to keep the patient protected and receiving appropriate services. However, I am saying that this mindset of "I have my rights" is highly destructive to marriage. We strong-willed wives must be careful to avoid this sense of entitlement. God does not grant you the privilege of life, liberty, and the pursuit of happiness, nor does He promise you a rose garden. He did not provide you with a marital bill of rights. Rather, He gave you a list of things that you are *required to do* for others. His Word stresses being the servant rather than the one being served.

## THE RESPONSIBILITIES OF MY JOB DESCRIPTION

God gives husbands and wives each a job description, not a bill of rights. Let's think about this as if we were applying for a job. A job description outlines the requirements and responsibilities of the job you are considering taking (before you sign on for the position). The description makes clear what your employer will expect of you. And although the job comes with privileges, such as pay and benefits, these privileges are not the focus of the job description. The job description is about what *you must do* to maintain the position, not what someone else is expected to do, and not what you will receive, deserve, or have the right to as a result of your position.

When you were considering taking on the job of being a husband or wife, did you examine the job description? It was available through Scripture, but how many of us took time to study it? And if we studied it at all, we likely paid much more attention to our spouse's job description than our own. But once we entered into that final contract, regardless of whether or not we read and understood our personal job description, we were saying that we agreed to perform the duties of our job, to the best of our ability, "until death us do part."

It's like signing a contract without reading the contents. How many of us have loaded new software onto our computers and then just clicked "agree" when asked if we accept the terms of the contract? Now be honest. Most of us just click and go, because we are more interested in the game than in the rules for participation. Regardless of whether we read the terms of the agreement or not, we are responsible for what those terms say. The same is true for more important contracts: a car, a house, a credit card.

So what about marriage? Should we just agree and go? Many people do. They sign on, more interested in the game than the contract and job description—the rules of the game that, if broken, could eliminate them from the game altogether. Many couples don't even realize that there are rules to the relationship until they've broken so many of them that the game is no longer fun. They can't figure out what they did wrong or why they're on the verge of elimination. It's around that time that they run in search of the rule book.

Most of us never read the entire contract for our credit cards, homes, or cars—at least not until something goes wrong and we want to find out who's responsible. Then we go through it with a fine-tooth comb. And let's say we read it after the fact and find out something is our responsibility. Then what? Can we claim ignorance and hope that fixes it? Hardly. The rules were available. It was our responsibility to be familiar with them and to comply with them.

Have you ever tried telling a police officer, "I'm sorry, officer; I just didn't realize the speed limit through here"? I have, and I'm here to tell you, it doesn't work! And it won't work with your husband either. You should read, know, and comply with your job description as a wife. You'd expect the same of your husband. If you don't, you will suffer the consequences.

Many couples believe that their marriage is breaking down because "you didn't meet my needs." But the truth is, marriages break down because "I didn't do my job." I have seldom heard a couple say, "My marriage is falling apart, and I know it's because I'm not loving her the way God says I should," or "I'm here because I know I'm not submitting to my husband and respecting him the way God wants me to."

It's much more comfortable for each of us to focus on what the other person did or didn't do. As long as I concentrate on your failure to meet my needs, I'm not at fault. I can blame you and feel justified in my dissatisfaction. If I stopped focusing on you, I would have to look at what I haven't done and what I need to change. This change of focus is exactly what *must* occur. Unless we start taking personal responsibility for where we've fallen short of our God-given responsibilities, then our marriage will not heal. We can't change our spouse, but we can change ourselves, and that's where our attention needs to be.

When I share this with couples in counseling, I often get opposition. Wives say, "I couldn't do my job because he didn't do his." The finger pointing remains at the other person instead of at ourselves. Scripture tells us, "First take the plank out of your own eye, and then you will see clearly to remove the speck from your brother's eye" (Matthew 7:5). This Scripture needs to be applied much more often to our marital relationships. Instead of pointing out to our husband the ways he's falling short, we should concentrate on improving our own job performance.

I hope you will stop right now and take time to pray, asking God to . . .

- Make you aware of how you may have twisted Scripture in your own mind to make yourself more comfortable.
- Reveal to you when you attempt to focus more

on what you think you have the right to rather than on what you have the responsibility to give within marriage.

- Help you avoid thinking of what your husband needs to change and begin right now focusing on what parts of your job description you personally need to improve.


## WHAT ARE MY JOB RESPONSIBILITIES?

Even if you took on your job as a wife without first reading the job description, you are still responsible for it. So whether you know it all already or not, it's time to look at what you were supposed to be doing all along and start doing it—to get things moving in the right direction. Better late than never. In order to build a loving, intimate, Christ-centered marriage, you need to know what Christ expects from you.

Although our emphasis is on our own individual responsibilities as wives—no finger pointing at our husbands—let's review the job descriptions given to husbands and wives through Scripture.

As I see it, Scripture gives three distinct sets of responsibilities for relationships. I'll spend the next three chapters outlining these. This chapter looks at joint responsibilities that both the husband and wife are expected to fulfill. The next two chapters look at the husband's unique responsibilities and then the wife's.

As you read these chapters, focus on what applies to *you*, not your spouse. Instead of gathering additional ammunition about what your husband is doing wrong, ask God to reveal where you need to improve.

## JOINT RESPONSIBILITIES

Scripture tells us how we are to interact with each other. If you and your husband are both Christians, then you are not just husband and wife, but also brother and sister in Christ. Therefore, Scripture says how you should treat each other. Let's look at just a few of the responsibilities that all Christians have and, therefore, you as a Christian couple also have. Although these are guidelines for all relationships, we will focus on how they should play out within your marriage.

At the end of this section, I will ask that you prayerfully review the Scripture passages and ask God to evaluate your job performance. Be open to His showing you how well you are demonstrating these traits. Take your time, and allow God to speak.

*Love Each Other*

"My command is this: Love each other as I have loved you. Greater love has no one than this, that he lay down his life for his friends. . . . This is my command: Love each other." (John 15:12-13,17)

Love one another deeply, from the heart. (1 Peter 1:22)

Above all, love each other deeply, because love covers over a multitude of sins. (1 Peter 4:8)

This is the message you heard from the beginning: We should love one another. (1 John 3:11)

Love is an action, not a feeling. We are to let our actions toward our spouse show him and the world that we love him. If you have questions about how to show love to your spouse, check out 1 Corinthians 13. If you are still not sure what to do, I suggest asking your spouse what actions make him feel loved. He knows what he hopes for, so why not ask?

## Submit to Each Other

Submit to one another out of reverence for Christ. (Ephesians 5:21)

I urge you, brothers, to submit to such as these and to everyone who joins in the work, and labors at it. (1 Corinthians 16:15-16)

There we go, throwing around that "s" word. I know this is a very difficult concept for us as strong-willed wives to swallow. But this chapter is talking about the mutual submission that occurs between husbands and wives as well as all Christians. When both husband and wife are Christians, you are both commanded to submit to each other "out of reverence for Christ." If your husband is not a believer, chapter 11 has specifics just for you. Mutual submission is based on valuing one another as equals and is the key to harmony in all of our relationships, especially marriage. Mutual submission will grow as we choose to obey and glorify God. A natural fruit of growing closer to God and surrendering our lives to Him is that we become more willing to surrender our personal rights, needs, and desires. We begin to see others as greater than ourselves and become less self-centered. In marriage this mutual submission between believers can be at its best as we seek to serve each other out of our love for the other and for Christ.

## Be Kind and Compassionate to Each Other

Be kind and compassionate to one another.
(Ephesians 4:32)

Make sure that nobody pays back wrong for wrong,
but always try to be kind to each other and to
everyone else. (1 Thessalonians 5:15)

The Lord's servant must not quarrel; instead,
he must be kind to everyone, able to teach, not
resentful. (2 Timothy 2:24)

Do *kind* and *compassionate* describe the way you and
your spouse treat each other? Would your spouse agree?
What about your friends' observations of your marriage? Do
you treat your spouse as well as (or even better than) you do
a stranger on the street or a guest in your home? So often
our spouse gets the short end of the stick when it comes to
our kindness. Why do we give the best of ourselves to people
we hardly know and leave the leftovers for those we love the
most? Imagine how your marriage might change if you made
sure your husband got the best you had to give.

## Hold Each Other Accountable

If someone is caught in a sin, you who are spiritual
should restore him gently. (Galatians 6:1)

And we urge you, brothers, warn those who are idle,
encourage the timid, help the weak, be patient with
everyone. (1 Thessalonians 5:14)

Correct, rebuke and encourage—with great
patience and careful instruction. (2 Timothy 4:2)

Be very careful with this one! We are to hold each other
accountable and confront sin in order to restore others to
their relationships with God and fellow Christians. But when
a spouse speaks these words, they require an additional
dose of love and gentleness. Hearing any type of correction
or rebuke is almost always hard. As strong-willed wives, we
resist receiving these comments at just about any cost, but
even more so when they come from our husbands. But at the
same time, we strong-willed wives are quick (often too quick)
to give a rebuke or criticism, and we don't usually take the
time to consider how we say it. So an extra dose of love is
required along with a side of "think before you speak." James
reminds us to "be quick to listen, slow to speak" (1:19).

*Encourage and Edify Each Other*

Therefore encourage one another and build
each other up, just as in fact you are doing.
(1 Thessalonians 5:11)

Encourage one another daily, as long as it is called
Today, so that none of you may be hardened by sin's
deceitfulness. (Hebrews 3:13)

Let us consider how we may spur one another on
toward love and good deeds. (Hebrews 10:24)

Do not let any unwholesome talk come out of your
mouths, but only what is helpful for building others

up according to their needs, that it may benefit those who listen. (Ephesians 4:29)

The power of words! They can build up or tear down another person's sense of worth. To edify your spouse means to build him up, encourage him, enhance his self-esteem, and accept him as he is. You also encourage and edify by showing your appreciation for what he does for you. So often the things our spouse does for us on a daily basis go unnoticed or unappreciated. Take time every day to tell him how much you appreciate him. Tell him what you like about him. It's always nice to hear what someone else likes about us. Positive words reinforce a healthy self-esteem. We must learn to focus more on the positives than the negatives and remember to tell our husbands how much they mean to us.

*Confess Your Sins and Forgive Each Other*

Confess your sins to each other and pray for each other so that you may be healed. (James 5:16)

Bear with each other and forgive whatever grievances you may have against one another. Forgive as the Lord forgave you. (Colossians 3:13)

"For if you forgive men when they sin against you, your heavenly Father will also forgive you. But if you do not forgive men their sins, your Father will not forgive your sins." (Matthew 6:14-15)

"If your brother sins, rebuke him, and if he repents, forgive him. If he sins against you seven times in a day, and seven times comes back to you and says, 'I repent,' forgive him." (Luke 17:3-4)

This is an especially difficult one for us strong-willed wives. It's not that we think we're perfect and never make mistakes (although we may believe we come close). It's just that we don't like to focus on our failures and would rather move on and find a way to make it right, without having to confess to being wrong. But the Bible teaches that we are supposed to confess to being wrong and to seek forgiveness.

We also must forgive. That's another difficult concept for us. Once we feel hurt, we feel justified in making sure the person who hurt us (and sometimes everyone else too) knows just how bad we've been hurt. We tend to focus more on blaming and ridiculing than on forgiving. This will be an important place for us to allow God to work in us and mature us.

### Serve Each Other

"In everything, do to others what you would have them do to you, for this sums up the Law and the Prophets." (Matthew 7:12)

Serve one another in love. (Galatians 5:13)

Each one should use whatever gift he has received to serve others, faithfully administering God's grace in its various forms. (1 Peter 4:10)

Learning to be servant-minded can take practice for all of us, but especially for strong-willed wives who are often more self-serving than any of us wish to admit. As we identify our talents, we should want to use them for the betterment of our marriages and families. We are each gifted differently, and a healthy marriage will allow each spouse to use his or her God-given talents to benefit the marriage. We need to be careful not to divide responsibilities based on what society and stereotypes tell us. Instead, we should actively identify what each of us is good at and then use those skills to serve each other. (More will be said on this in chapter 17.) Are you using your gifts to the best of your ability within your marriage?

*Live in Peace and Unity with Each Other*

How good and pleasant it is when brothers live together in unity! (Psalm 133:1)

May the God who gives endurance and encouragement give you a spirit of unity among yourselves as you follow Christ Jesus, so that with one heart and mouth you may glorify the God and Father of our Lord Jesus Christ. (Romans 15:5-6)

I appeal to you, brothers, in the name of our Lord Jesus Christ, that all of you agree with one another so that there may be no divisions among you and that you may be perfectly united in mind and thought. (1 Corinthians 1:10)

Live in peace with each other. (1 Thessalonians 5:13)

Make every effort to live in peace with all men and to be holy; without holiness no one will see the Lord. (Hebrews 12:14)

Living in peace and unity is as close to experiencing oneness as we will ever have on earth. It requires that all the other descriptors of this job be met. It is the ultimate in surrendering our personal wants, needs, and desires to the greater good of everyone around us. Oneness is the opposite of self-centeredness and an ultimate joy to experience. We may not experience this in our marriages every day, but we should always strive to get a little closer to this ideal. Our selfish natures rob us of this experience. But as we surrender more and more of ourselves to Christ, we will get closer to living in peace and unity.

## A PERFORMANCE EVALUATION

The requirements of your job description are listed below. Take a few minutes to review the verses listed in this chapter that describe what God intends you to do, and then prayerfully answer how well you have been doing. Focus on your own completion of these responsibilities and don't worry about your husband's performance. Circle the number that best represents how completely you meet each descriptor.

1=Excellent   2=Above Average   3=Average
4=Below Average   5=Poor

| | | | | |
|---|---|---|---|---|
| Love each other | 1 | 2 | 3 | 4 | 5 |
| Submit to each other | 1 | 2 | 3 | 4 | 5 |
| Be kind and compassionate | 1 | 2 | 3 | 4 | 5 |
| Hold each other accountable | 1 | 2 | 3 | 4 | 5 |
| Encourage and edify each other | 1 | 2 | 3 | 4 | 5 |

| Confess sins and forgive | 1 | 2 | 3 | 4 | 5 |
| Serve each other | 1 | 2 | 3 | 4 | 5 |
| Live in peace and unity | 1 | 2 | 3 | 4 | 5 |

How well are you fulfilling this portion of the job description? Did you earn a raise, get a pat on the back, receive a gentle reprimand, get placed on ninety-day probation, or maybe fail every day and deserve to lose your job? Thankfully, God is merciful and patient. He will help us learn to perform our jobs to the best of our abilities. Let's each hope our husband is almost as merciful and patient with us (and we with him).

I know that the above exercise may have been painful for you. It was for me. But there is hope. Now that we have let God search our hearts, we can be open to His guidance as He helps us make the necessary changes to be more obedient to His commands. Take time right now to pray and ask God to forgive you for where you have fallen short and to give you the strength and insight to change.

**COMING UP NEXT**

Having looked at our joint responsibilities in marriage, we will look next at the job responsibilities God has assigned to our husbands. We should read these not only as what he should do, but also as what we are supposed to allow him to do. Although some of these responsibilities would be good coming from us as well, many of them are simply not our jobs. And as long as we are doing them for ourselves, we make it difficult for our husband to fulfill his God-given roles.

# CHAPTER 9

# As Christ Loved the Church: A Husband's Responsibilities

IN THE LAST CHAPTER we learned about the responsibilities that each of us, as Christians, has to one another. These are things we are to do in every one of our relationships with other believers. But specific responsibilities are given only to husband and wife. In this and the following chapter, we will look more closely at the specific responsibilities within marriage. The responsibilities of husband and wife are designed to meet our particular needs as a male or female. You'll notice that the responsibilities the Bible sets forth for men seem to be exactly what we wives say we need. And the responsibilities set forth biblically to wives (chapter 10) will meet our husbands' strongest needs. Isn't it great how the Creator of marriage really does know how it will work best and has given the specific instructions needed to make your spouse feel treasured?

We've talked about how many of us strong-willed wives have a tendency to rehash old hurts and ways we feel others have wronged us. As you read about how God has chosen for your husband to relate to you in marriage, focus on your gratitude to God for His own unconditional love and provision.

I hope your husband will read this chapter along with you. Because this chapter is specifically about his responsibilities, I will speak directly to him as we discuss them.

## A HUSBAND'S RESPONSIBILITIES

The specific responsibilities that God gives to a husband are his and his alone. These unique requirements are to be fulfilled only in the job as husband. These are *not* roles that God has given to every man in relation to every woman. Rather, these are roles given to a husband to perform in his relationship with his wife.

There's only one responsibility Scripture assigns uniquely to husbands and that is to "love your wives, just as Christ loved the church" (Ephesians 5:25). All other requirements are encompassed in that one command. At first glance it may seem easy to say you have only one responsibility. However, a closer look shows how difficult your job is. This one statement involves many behaviors. God knew marriage relationships would be difficult for us and wanted to give us as much help as possible.

Again, first the apostle Paul tells husbands to "love your wives, just as Christ loved the church and gave himself up for her" (Ephesians 5:25). In verse 28 he goes on, "In this same way, husbands ought to love their wives as their own bodies." As Christ loved the church and as a man loves his own body—those are big shoes to fill. Just how did Christ show His love for the church?

## WHEN ALL ELSE FAILS, READ THE INSTRUCTIONS

I know that when working on many projects you may throw the instructions across the room, saying, "I don't need those. This looks simple enough—I can figure it out myself." But I hope in this case you will understand the importance of not only keeping the instruction Book close by, but studying it closely. This thing called marriage is far more complex and puzzling than any "some assembly required" toy on Christmas Eve. So let's study the Bible's instructions and find some examples of how Christ demonstrated His love for us. These will be your model for how to love your wife.

**CHRIST DEMONSTRATED HIS LOVE
BY SERVING HER (THE CHURCH)**

One of the most beautiful pictures in Scripture is that of Jesus kneeling in front of His disciples and washing their feet. It was a servant's job to wash the feet of guests. But in John 13 we see Jesus—Messiah, Lord of lords, and King of kings—taking the position of a servant to show the depth of His love. John wrote, "Having loved his own who were in the world, he now showed them the full extent of his love" (verse 1). He loved them so much that He was willing to humble Himself and serve them.

Husband, how often do you serve your wife? I don't mean by washing her feet (although that may not be a bad idea). I'm not referring to times when you do a household task just to get her off your back, or help her with the children with the hope that it will give her more energy for after-the-kids-go-to-bed activities. Serving her as Christ served cannot come with strings attached, alternative agendas, or a guilty or angry heart. It must come out of your love for her and your desire to show her how much you treasure her. If she is the most important person on earth to you, you should treat her as such.

The ways you can serve your wife are limited only by your imagination. Your current circumstances give you a long list of tasks that can ease a wife's overload. You can assume household duties, fix her a special dinner, take over the kids' bath time, encourage her to read her favorite magazine, or do the grocery shopping. Or maybe put gas in her car, open doors for her, give her your jacket when she's cold, or rub her back. Then you might want to consider washing her hair, painting her fingernails, and shaving her legs for her—okay, maybe I hit a limit here. But the point is that if your heart desires to love your wife above all others, then there are many ways to show her how much you love her through serving her.

## CHRIST DEMONSTRATED HIS LOVE BY PROVIDING FOR HER NEEDS

Scripture contains example after example of God's desire to provide for His people's needs. Jesus was keenly aware of the needs of His disciples and of the crowds who followed Him. He acted by first meeting the physical and emotional needs of people before reaching them spiritually.

*Jesus met physical needs by:*

- Providing food: Matthew 15:32-38; Mark 8:1-13
- Doing all He could for those who were sick: Matthew 9:27-30; Luke 4:38-39; 8:43-48
- Encouraging rest: Mark 6:31; Matthew 11:28
- Healing the sick: Luke 4:38-39; 8:43-48

*Jesus met emotional needs by:*

- Relieving fears: Matthew 8:23-27; 14:26-27

- Lifting burdens: Matthew 11:28-30
- Providing comfort: John 14:1-4
- Relieving worry: Matthew 6:25-34

*Jesus met intellectual needs by:*

- Teaching, teaching, and more teaching: Matthew 5–7; Mark 1:21-22; Luke 20:20-26; John 3:1-21; 7:14-17
- Talking and explaining: Matthew 16:21; Mark 4:34; Luke 24:32

*Jesus met spiritual needs by:*

- Praying for people: Matthew 19:13; John 17:20-26
- Speaking forgiveness: Matthew 9:1-8; Mark 2:5; Luke 7:48; 23:34

Paul also speaks to this issue of providing for your wife's needs in Ephesians 5:28-30: "In this same way, husbands ought to love their wives as their own bodies. He who loves his wife loves himself. After all, no one ever hated his own body, but he feeds and cares for it, just as Christ does the church—for we are members of his body." He "feeds" it, or in the King James Version, he "nourisheth" his body. Nourishing one's body refers to providing for all the body's needs, not just food. Nourishing your wife also means much more than bringing home a paycheck and providing financially. Although that is a very important part of nourishing, it's not enough. Too many men feel they've done all they're required to do if they simply hold down a job and make sure the bills are paid. Yet nourishing your wife also includes providing for her emotional, intellectual, and spiritual needs.

Paul rebukes any man who doesn't provide for his family: "If anyone does not provide for his relatives, and especially for his immediate family, he has denied the faith and is worse than an unbeliever" (1 Timothy 5:8). That's strong language. A man who doesn't provide is "worse than an unbeliever." Men, I strongly encourage you to take time to evaluate how well you're doing in providing for your wife—really providing according to God's standards. Don't stop short of all that God has called you to do. You must not only meet her physical needs of food, clothing, and shelter, but also her emotional, intellectual, and spiritual needs. She needs you to comfort her when she's hurt or scared, talk and listen to her, and serve as the spiritual leader of your home. You can't be the only one to meet her emotional and spiritual needs—friends and other Christians also have roles in her life—but you shouldn't count on others to do your part.

Have you been providing for what your wife needs? Can she become the most physically healthy, best educated, most emotionally well-adjusted, and most spiritually mature woman she can possibly be? I understand that you are married to a strong-willed woman, and she often tells you she doesn't need you. But the truth is, she does! Whether she'll admit it or not, she does! When she fights you on this or simply doesn't let you take the lead in this area, lovingly remind her that God told you to care for her.

## CHRIST DEMONSTRATED HIS LOVE BY BEING HER PROTECTOR

What image comes to your mind when you think of a shepherd and his sheep? Close your eyes and imagine. . . . Oh, wait, you can't close your eyes and keep reading, so let me visualize for you. I see a beautiful green pasture filled with fluffy white sheep grazing quietly. The sky is blue, the sun is shining, and there is a gentle breeze. The shepherd stands by a tree on a small hill nearby. He is watchful, on alert. But why? Everything seems so peaceful. Why doesn't he just lie down and relax? Why not take a nap or look for pictures in the clouds as they float by? Those sheep seem to be taking care of themselves just fine. What is he there for anyway? Talk about an easy job—right? Wrong!

The shepherd knows that danger is everywhere. His sheep could be harmed if he doesn't pay attention. He's there to protect them. Here's how Jesus describes Himself:

> "I am the good shepherd. The good shepherd lays down his life for the sheep. The hired hand is not the shepherd who owns the sheep. So when he sees the wolf coming, he abandons the sheep and runs away. Then the wolf attacks the flock and scatters it. The man runs away because he is a hired hand and cares nothing for the sheep.
>
> "I am the good shepherd; I know my sheep and my sheep know me—just as the Father knows me and I know the Father—and I lay down my life for the sheep. . . . No one takes it from me, but I lay it down of my own accord." (John 10:11-15,18)

As the Good Shepherd, Jesus is our ultimate protector. He loves us and will do all He can to protect us from harm. As a husband, are you protecting your wife? Would you describe yourself as a "good shepherd" or are you more like the "hired hand"? Or maybe a better question would be, which would your wife say you are? Are you doing all you can to keep her out of harm's way? Are you protecting her physically by making sure the place she lives in and the car she drives are safe? Are you protecting her emotionally by standing up for her, validating her feelings, and keeping harsh words from coming toward her (including words from your own mouth)? Are you protecting her spiritually by praying for her? Or are you using her strong-willed nature and independence as an excuse to abdicate your responsibilities?

Jesus said we are to follow His example. Learn to protect your wife. You may encounter some resistance from her. We strong-willed wives don't always respond appropriately to a husband's attempts to protect us, because we don't think we need protecting. We think we have it all under control. We may interpret attempts to protect us as saying we are too weak to take care of ourselves. That's not something we often believe about ourselves, so we're likely to get irritated. But if your wife responds defensively, just lovingly remind her that you love her and want to protect her. Not because she's incapable of protecting herself, but because you don't want her to *have* to protect herself. She will gradually see and appreciate your protective arms.

My husband, Jim, and I have struggled with this protection concept. He has always tried to protect me; it's just his nature. However, I haven't always accepted his protection. At times I have actually refused it, because "I'm a big girl, and I can take care of myself!" I don't know that I evaluated whether I wanted to take care of myself; I just knew I could. And when he tried to protect me, I thought I had to prove to him that I didn't need it. Over time, it dawned on me that maybe he wasn't protecting me because he thought I needed it; it was more about what he needed. He *needed* to be my protector. It was his God-given role to protect and care for those he loved, and I wasn't letting him. This realization has helped me to more easily accept his efforts to protect me. I've found that I like being protected, no longer having to stand out there alone just to prove I can.

Paul addressed protection when he spoke of how a man loves his own body in that he "feeds and *cares for* it" (Ephesians 5:29, emphasis added). What does it mean to "care for" your body? It has to do with all those little extras we do for ourselves. Maybe they aren't life-and-death issues like food and water, but they show we care about ourselves. We take vitamins, shower daily, brush our teeth, and exercise. We spend time with friends and pursue hobbies. If something is important to us, we'll care for it. We'll go beyond the bare essentials and pamper it. The word I like to use most in this area is *treasuring*. We should not only treasure our bodies, but even more important, we should treasure our spouse. If you truly treasure your wife, you'll protect her.

To treasure something means to view it as of great value. Something that you dreamed of, worked for, and finally received. A priceless gift. Something you're thankful for and never take for granted. We know how to maintain and care for our car, house, or other valuables. But we have been given a much more valuable gift, one that we often treat with little concern: our spouse. We should treat our spouse better than any material possession, and according to Scripture, as well as we treat our own bodies.

Husband, are you obeying Scripture by caring for your wife as well as you do yourself? Are you treasuring her? Are you putting as much effort into caring for and protecting her as you did your first or favorite automobile? Do you take time to pamper her, shield her from harm, and encourage her?

## CHRIST DEMONSTRATED HIS LOVE
## BY SACRIFICING FOR HER

Christ loved His bride, the church, so much that He was willing to lay down His life for her. The purpose of this sacrifice was not to become a martyr or to bring glory to Himself. Rather, it was "to make her holy, cleansing her by the washing with water through the word, and to present her to himself as a radiant church, without stain or wrinkle or any other blemish, but holy and blameless" (Ephesians 5:26-27). The sacrifice was about *her* spiritual well-being. He was willing to do whatever He had to do to make sure she was where she needed to be spiritually.

Are you following Christ's example? Are you doing everything in your power to make sure your wife is spiritually whole? I'm not saying it's your responsibility to "save" her or to make her study her Bible. But it is your responsibility to do everything you possibly can—even if it means sacrificing something yourself—to provide her with what she needs to grow spiritually. Are you being the spiritual leader of your home by:

- interceding on her behalf?
- praying for her daily?
- providing instruction from God's Word to your children?
- sharing your insights on Scripture and creating an atmosphere where she is free to do this also?
- modeling a life growing closer to God?
- initiating couple quiet time and prayer?
- allowing her time in her schedule for Bible study and personal quiet time?

Having a sacrificial love for your wife also means putting her needs before your own. It means making her a priority in your life and making her happiness as important as your own. My husband has always lived by this motto: God first, others (especially me and the children) second, and self third. He has shown by example that he is more than willing to put his personal needs and wants on the back burner to meet his family's needs and desires. He has often turned down a golf game, card night with the guys, or just time to get the yard mowed in order to give me time to write, spend time with friends, or go to Wal-Mart by myself (which is a major treat in my mind).

I'm not saying that husbands shouldn't have time for themselves — they definitely should. What I am saying is that you need an attitude of selflessness more than selfishness.

I counseled a couple who were struggling with this very issue. The wife came into the first therapy session alone. As she sat down, she sighed. When I asked how she was feeling, she said, "Relieved to be here by myself. This is the first time in almost two months that I've had any time to myself. I think I just want to sit here and enjoy it." I thought, *How sad that she has to come to therapy in order to get any time alone.*

As we talked, I learned she had two preschool children and stayed with them while her husband went to work. He had made it clear that he expected her to run errands during the day so that once he got home they could have "family time." And weekends were focused on his relaxing from his hard week at work and doing yard work, and her needing to keep the kids quiet so he could prepare for his Sunday school lesson. She knew he loved her and the kids but didn't feel they were much of a priority to him. She couldn't recall the last time he had asked her what she needed or how he could help her. She felt guilty complaining about him, because he really was a great guy and provided well for his family. She felt she was being selfish if she asked him to watch the kids so she could spend time with friends or get her hair cut. "After all, I guess I do have all day to do things like that."

I helped her understand that healthy families work to strike a balance in areas of self time, family time, couple time, work time, and so on. These were not balanced in her home. Over the next couple of months, she and her husband attended therapy together and learned to better meet each other's needs. This happened in part as her husband became aware of some selfish tendencies and began to replace them with an understanding of sacrificial love.

## CHRIST DEMONSTRATED HIS LOVE
## BY BEING GENTLE AND HUMBLE

Throughout His earthly ministry, Christ modeled a gentle spirit. He described Himself in this way: "Take my yoke upon you and learn from me, for I am gentle and humble in heart, and you will find rest for your souls" (Matthew 11:29). Jesus was easy to learn from because He was gentle. Husbands, have you ever tried to teach your wife something only to end up in an argument? If you are married to a strong-willed wife, I suspect the answer to that question is a resounding *yes*! I know we strong-willed women can be hard to teach at times. But before you assume it's all our problem, consider whether your presentation met with Christ's example. Were you gentle with your words and attitudes as you tried to teach?

Sometimes Jesus chose to rebuke or confront someone. But even in these instances, He was gentle. He didn't raise His voice to yell at the person who had done something wrong. Whenever He disagreed, challenged, advised, or taught those around Him, He spoke the truth with love, not anger. Matthew quoted the prophet Isaiah, who said of the Messiah, "He will not quarrel or cry out; no one will hear his voice in the streets" (Matthew 12:19). When things upset Jesus, He controlled His emotions. He was not harsh or judgmental. Even in His strongest rebukes as recorded in Matthew 23, He did not call names unnecessarily or make degrading comments out of spite or rage. He did not intimidate, and He did not yell. Has your voice ever been "heard in the streets"? Maybe you've never been that loud, but if you can't maintain your composure and end up raising your voice to your wife, you're not following Christ's example.

Jesus was not only gentle in His dealings with people, He was also humble in His attitude. Although He was God and King, He didn't use that position to put Himself above others. He didn't bring attention to Himself or try to prove He was right. He was secure in who He was and therefore wasn't out to prove anything to anyone. He served others without pride getting in the way. He said, "For even the Son of Man did not come to be served, but to serve" (Mark 10:45), and "For who is greater, the one who is at the table or the one who serves? Is it not the one who is at the table? But I am among you as one who serves" (Luke 22:27).

How would others describe you? Are you gentle in your teaching and rebuking? Are you humble, or do you strive to be the center of attention? Do you put your wife down whether in private or in public? Is your wife drawn to your sweet spirit or repulsed by your selfish pride? Are you considerate of her?

Peter wrote, "Husbands, in the same way be considerate as you live with your wives, and treat them with respect as the weaker partner and as heirs with you of the gracious gift of life, so that nothing will hinder your prayers" (1 Peter 3:7).

## CHRIST DEMONSTRATED HIS LOVE
## BY PRAYING FOR HER

In John 17 we find an up-close-and-personal look at Jesus' prayer life. It is a beautiful example of how much He loves us. It takes place on the night of His arrest before His crucifixion. He knows He is about to be betrayed and will soon die a horrible death. At a time like that, most of us would pray for ourselves. Jesus does that, but then He takes time to pray for those He is leaving behind. He asks God the Father to protect those He loves—from the world and from the Evil One. He also says He wants those He loves to be in unity. How humbled we should be to know that just before His arrest, He takes time to put others' needs before His own.

Husbands, are you praying for your wife? Even when things are going badly and you feel like your life is a shambles and falling apart around you? Even when you're stressed out about your job? Even when you're sick? Are you taking time to pray not only for yourself but also for your wife?

I encourage you to sit down with your wife and ask her how you can best pray for her. Find out in what areas your wife feels she needs extra strength, where she feels she is struggling, and how she is asking God to work in and through her. Write these down as part of your prayer list, and commit to joining her in praying for the things that are important to her.

## CHRIST DEMONSTRATED HIS LOVE
## BY FORGIVING HER

More valuable than anything else Jesus could have given us, He gave us forgiveness of sins. Regardless of what it cost Him, He forgave. Choosing to forgive caused Jesus to be ridiculed, called names, threatened, scourged, and eventually killed.

He commands us to forgive as we have been forgiven. That means *no strings attached.* It means no longer holding it against the other person and definitely not reminding her about whatever she's done that hurt you. It means letting go of the past and holding on to a brighter future together.

When you're met with the challenge to forgive, remember that you too are a sinner who messes up. Ask yourself if you want your wife holding on to the things you've done to hurt her. (She may do this, and she needs to work on that, but that's not your responsibility.) Or better yet, do you want God to remember even one thing that you've done to hurt Him? Once we put forgiveness in this perspective, it's easier to grant. And regardless of how easy or difficult it may be to do, it's a command, not an option.

## IT'S TIME TO EVALUATE YOURSELF

Now that you've reviewed the responsibilities of your job description, it's time for a performance evaluation. I encourage you to spend a few minutes in prayer, seeking God and asking Him to open your eyes to see how you measure up to what He's expecting of you as a godly husband. Tell Him your desire to grow in Christlikeness and your willingness to see yourself as He sees you. Take a few minutes to review this chapter, then go through the section below, rating your-self on how well you're currently doing in each category. Use this as a measuring stick to help you know where you need the most improvement. You may want to come back to it after you have worked on each area for a while and see how much you've grown.

Here's a challenge if you are brave and would like feed-back to help you grow. Make a copy of this evaluation and give it to your wife. Ask her to evaluate your job performance and give you feedback on where you are doing well and where you still need to improve.

## MY PERSONAL JOB PERFORMANCE EVALUATION

Take time to prayerfully rate yourself on each of the following categories.

### I Demonstrate My Love for My Wife by Serving Her

| 1 | 2 | 3 | 4 | 5 |
|---|---|---|---|---|
| Never Demonstrate | | Sometimes Demonstrate | | Almost Always Demonstrate |

### I Demonstrate My Love for My Wife by Providing for Her Needs

| 1 | 2 | 3 | 4 | 5 |
|---|---|---|---|---|
| Never Demonstrate | | Sometimes Demonstrate | | Almost Always Demonstrate |

## I Demonstrate My Love for My Wife
## by Being Her Protector

| 1 | 2 | 3 | 4 | 5 |
|---|---|---|---|---|
| Never Demonstrate | | Sometimes Demonstrate | | Almost Always Demonstrate |

## I Demonstrate My Love for My Wife
## by Sacrificing for Her

| 1 | 2 | 3 | 4 | 5 |
|---|---|---|---|---|
| Never Demonstrate | | Sometimes Demonstrate | | Almost Always Demonstrate |

## I Demonstrate My Love for My Wife
## by Being Gentle and Humble

| 1 | 2 | 3 | 4 | 5 |
|---|---|---|---|---|
| Never Demonstrate | | Sometimes Demonstrate | | Almost Always Demonstrate |

## I Demonstrate My Love for My Wife
## by Praying for Her

| 1 | 2 | 3 | 4 | 5 |
|---|---|---|---|---|
| Never Demonstrate | | Sometimes Demonstrate | | Almost Always Demonstrate |

## I Demonstrate My Love for My Wife
## by Forgiving Her

| 1 | 2 | 3 | 4 | 5 |
|---|---|---|---|---|
| Never Demonstrate | | Sometimes Demonstrate | | Almost Always Demonstrate |

## COMING UP NEXT

Wives, I'm speaking to you again now: We've delayed as long as we can. We've talked about joint responsibilities and our husbands' job description, and now it's finally our turn. In the next chapter we are going face what God has instructed (commanded really) us wives to do. This is not Debbie or anyone else telling you what you need to do. It is simply looking into God's Word and identifying those verses that specifically apply to us. If you are anything like me, these instructions come from the very verses that we strong-willed wives work hard to avoid and forget. But now it's time to let God tell us what we need to do to truly honor Him within our marriage.

# CHAPTER 10

# As to the Lord:
# A Wife's Responsibilities

OKAY, WOMEN, NOW IT'S our turn. We also have a job description and set of responsibilities to perform in our marriage. As a matter of fact, our job description begins clear back at the beginning: Genesis. We were created as a result of a void that needed to be filled. Something was missing, and our first mother's responsibility was to fill that void.

Have you ever created anything? Painted a house, drawn a picture, planted a garden? Don't you just love that feeling of surveying your creation and thinking, "Wow, that looks really great!" But, what if that's not your reaction? What if, as you step back, you see that something is missing? A section of the house that got missed, a part of the painting you forgot to put in, or a whole row of carrots that didn't get planted. What would you do? Would you say, "Oh, it's not that big a deal. I just want to be done," or would you get right back in there and finish the job?

We can imagine that that's what happened to God. At the end of a long, hard week of creating the universe, God sat back on the fluffiest La-Z-Boy cloud He could find and reviewed His creation. He looked at what He had accomplished and decided it was good. But as He sat there watching Adam name the animals as they paraded by, He knew something very important was missing. "And Adam gave names to all cattle, and to the fowl of the air, and to every beast of the field; but for Adam there was not found an help meet for him" (Genesis 2:20, KJV).

God immediately started working to fix the problem. He put Adam into a deep sleep, removed a rib, and formed Eve — the completion not only of creation, but also of man in the image of God. He made a "help meet" (KJV) for Adam.

## WHAT IS A "HELP MEET"?

I always wondered what the words *help meet* meant. I believed it meant to be a "helper," because that's the word in translations of the Bible other than King James. But as I dug in and studied this, I realized that this is not just any helper. It's a "suitable helper" (NIV). I see a difference. I am not here to help Jim just like anyone else in the world could help him. As his wife, I have been created to "suit" him. If you hear someone say, "motherhood really suits her," or "marriage suits you," what are they saying? They mean that it complements who she is, it brings out the best in her. I think that's what God intended Eve to do for Adam, and what He intends each of us to do for our husbands. We are to be helpers that complement or complete who he is and bring out the best in him.

I know that many strong-willed women are offended at being referred to as a man's "helper," regardless of how "suitable" we are. We see a "helper" as inferior to whomever we are helping. But I'd like you to reconsider that reaction. The term translated as "helper" refers to a beneficial relationship where one person aids or supports another as a friend and ally. The reason I don't believe we should be offended by this term is because of who else this word is used to describe. The same word for "help" is used to describe *God*: "God is our refuge and strength, an ever-present help in trouble" (Psalm 46:1). I'd say He's pretty good company. And since God is not seen as inferior, neither should women, or wives in this case, be.

I have heard a modern use of the term *help meet* that gives a beautiful word picture. It is a construction term. A column of a building can be made stronger by adding additional material around the original column. The new material placed around the column strengthens the column so it can support extra weight or stress, and is called a "help meet." In this usage, *help meet* means to "surround" and "to support by surrounding." The help meet actually gives additional strength to the original structure.

What a beautiful way of thinking about our role as wives. God didn't create us to be slaves or bosses, but through our presence to strengthen and support our husbands. We complement and bring out the best in our husbands so that the two of us, together as one flesh, are stronger and able to accomplish more than either could alone.

This concept became very real to me through a nearly disastrous experience at my home. Jim was painting our vaulted foyer. I was helping here and there on the lower sections but spent most of my time keeping three kids and a dog from running under the ladder or through the paint. Once the lower sections were finished, it was time to climb the smaller of two ladders. Because I'm terrified of heights, I knew I'd be no help there. As a matter of fact, I don't even like seeing anyone else on a ladder and hate having to look up to see what he's doing. Even with my feet firmly planted on the ground, I was of little use to Jim because I got shaky just looking up to hand him a rag. So the kids and I ran off and left Jim on his own.

He continued working until he had reached as high as he could from the top of a six-foot stepladder. But this only got him a little over halfway up the twenty-four-foot walls. So out came the extension ladder. Knowing I was mush just sitting on the stairs watching him, he rigged up some amazing way to keep that ladder in place. But eventually he had no choice but to ask for my help. He had to reach some of the highest peaks, and the ladder wasn't secure enough for his comfort. So he enlisted me to do nothing more than hold the bottom of the ladder. "You don't even have to look up," he said. "Just lean against the ladder to keep it more stable as I stand at the top." How hard could that be?

So there I was, leaning against the ladder, refusing to look up and see what crazy position he had placed his body in to reach as far as he could. I was attempting to concentrate on the kids to keep from thinking about what was going on fifteen feet above me. The next thing I knew, Talon, our two-year-old, came wiggling into the foyer with his legs tightly held together and a grimace on his face that immediately told Mom to grab him and run for the potty. So I did.

At least, I started to. I had only gotten as far as picking Talon up and taking two steps when I heard a blood-curdling scream from somewhere in the heavens. I looked up, wondering what in the world could be making such a racket. And there I saw my wonderful husband panicking as the ladder began sliding down the wall and out from under him. Without thinking I dropped Talon and grabbed the ladder in the nick of time. (Talon had an accident, but a much easier one to clean up than the one Jim might have had.)

The sliding of the ladder was stopped, but not the

pounding of either of our hearts. Jim hurried down the ladder, and I grabbed him to apologize. But what do you say after something like that? "Hey, sorry, I just didn't think my standing there was all that important." Or, "I guess I just forgot you were up there, sorry." I think I tried both of those, but neither made much difference after he had just had his life flash before his eyes.

Jim did eventually forgive me for trying to kill him and finished painting over the claw marks in the wall (which I'm sure you can still see if you want to climb up there to look—I'll even hold the ladder for you). As scary as this experience was, I came away from it with a wonderful example of what a "help meet" is.

Jim had done as much as he could on his own. He had reached as high and far as one person could reach. He had even climbed the ladder as far as he felt safe to climb. But he had reached his limit. With my help, my support of the ladder, he was able to reach higher and accomplish more than he could have without me, his help meet. Even though I didn't think my presence was all that important, I found out differently. As soon as I removed my support, he began to fall.

Being a help meet is not about being inferior. It is about being there to support your husband so he can reach the full potential that God created him to reach. It doesn't mean you won't also be allowed to do the things God created you to do. It simply means that you don't get so wrapped up in reaching for your own goals that your husband and marriage suffer.

## RESPECT

Peter wrote that we are to "Show proper respect to everyone" (1 Peter 2:17). Paul applied this command to the marital relationship when he said, "and the wife must respect her husband" (Ephesians 5:33). Do you know what that means? I've often heard husbands say, "I just want her to respect me." But when I ask a husband specifically what that means to him or how his wife could show it, he is usually at a loss for words. Not because he doesn't know it when he sees it, but because it's such a difficult concept to describe. God gave us, as wives, the command to respect our husbands, but do we understand this command well enough to obey it?

Webster's defines *respect* as "to hold in high esteem, honor or reverence; to treat with consideration."[1] Those are strong words. How do you think your husband would feel if you applied that definition to him every day? What if you were to actually hold him in high esteem? Or show reverence for him and treat him with consideration?

Why don't we do this every day? He deserves it (well, usually). And regardless of whether he deserves it, God Himself commands us to do it. It's not an option on our part or a reward for good behavior on his part. It's the way we're supposed to treat him each and every day.

Showing respect for your husband means that you give him the absolute best part of yourself. The best of your attitude, your time, your language, your dress, your gifts—the best everything. So often our husband ends up with our leftovers, not our best. Do you treat your husband as well as you treat a causal acquaintance or even a stranger? It's sad that many of us show more consideration to a stranger than to the man we love. Respecting your husband means treating him with the same attention, attitude, and admiration as you would the President of the United States, the Queen of England, Billy Graham, or whomever you greatly admire.

Let's say you've had a really rotten day at work, got stuck

in traffic for an hour, and are generally in a bad mood by the time you reach home. Then, as you walk into your house, an old friend who you had completely forgotten was coming for dinner greets you. Let's say that old friend is none other than Jesus Christ. The frown on your face and the growl in your voice would quickly be replaced with a smile and pleasantries. You'd do your best to put the bad day behind you. You'd likely give Jesus a hug and tell Him how much you have missed Him and how glad you are to see Him.

How likely is it that your husband would receive that same greeting from you after the same kind of day? My guess is slim to none. But that's what we should strive for. Not that we can't talk about a bad day, but that we shouldn't take a bad day out on the ones we love.

Be sure your husband gets your best. Hold him in high esteem. Show respect to him in all you say and do every day. Be sure the way you talk to him (or about him) is honoring and considerate. Don't use hurtful or rough language with him, don't nag or criticize his efforts or lack of them, don't undermine his discipline of the children, and don't tease him about sensitive areas. Instead, encourage him, lift him up, affirm him, and show that you appreciate and admire him. Brag about him both to his face and behind his back. Seek out his advice and opinions. Show respect for his needs for both individuality and togetherness, and help to keep these balanced.

## SUBMISSION

I know, I know, we hate that word. But do we know what *submission* means? I thought I did, but I have since come to understand that my definition was largely a result of things

I had heard other people say, not fact from what God says. I was holding on to myths as to what submission required of me, and I fear that many of you are as well.

In the next two chapters we will address several of the myths that surround submission and discuss what God really meant. But now we simply need to understand that it is a command from Scripture that we must choose to follow if we want a marriage filled with blessings. We need to find out what God meant by submission and stop rejecting it because of what society says. When we reach chapters 11 and 12, I hope you will see that submission isn't a dirty word or a cruel joke played on us by a male-dominated culture, the patriarchs, or our heavenly Father. It is simply God's way of placing order in our lives to keep things running as smoothly as possible.

In Ephesians 5:22-24, Paul states what we are commanded to do:

Wives, submit to your husbands as to the Lord.
For the husband is the head of the wife as Christ
is the head of the church, his body, of which he is
the Savior. Now as the church submits to Christ,
so also wives should submit to their husbands in
everything.

Whether or not we like this, it is a God-given command, and in choosing not to obey the command, we are choosing to live in sin. There are consequences to sin. We obey the laws of this country not because we necessarily like every one of them. We obey them whether or not we like them. We obey because they were established by our authorities, are intended to protect us, and have penalties if we choose to break them. And God covered submission to instituted authority too (see 1 Peter 2:13-14). We should consider God's laws even more highly than those made by people. We should obey God's instructions whether we like them or not. We obey because they have been established by our ultimate authority, God the Father. He established them for our protection, and there are consequences for disobeying them. I believe many of us are experiencing consequences within our marriage as a result of our disobedience. And even more importantly, we are experiencing consequences in our relationship with God as a result of repetitive sin if we refuse to understand and practice true submission.

Wives are commanded to submit to their husbands. No matter how we slice it, a command is a command is a command. And according to Scripture, if we love our Lord Jesus Christ, we will obey His commands (see John 14:23). I believed with all my heart that I loved Him, was surrendered to Him, and would yield my will to His. (Well, at least once I found I couldn't change His mind.) Then it happened. Jesus, in His ever-so-gentle and loving way, dropped a ton of bricks in my lap and told me to reevaluate my life.

It happened on one of my writing and researching days. As I was reading about submission in one of the many books I had collected, I read, "Your attitude toward your husband reveals your spiritual condition. You are rebellious to Christ's leadership to the same degree that you rebel against your husband's leadership."[2] Ouch! *No, this couldn't be right! I loved and served Jesus with all my heart. What does that have to do with rebellion and submission toward Jim? I know I don't always (okay, hardly ever) let Jim be the leader of our home, but that doesn't stop me from loving and submitting to Jesus. I AM NOT REBELLING AGAINST JESUS!*

I had never put these two attitudes together. I knew my heart was to surrender to God's will. I prayed for less of me and more of Him. I prayed for His guidance and said I was willing to follow where He led me. How dare this author tell me I wasn't being submissive to my Savior just because I was not submitting to my husband? As my shock turned to what I thought was righteous anger, I decided she must be wrong. I went to Scripture and began searching for truth.

I knew submission was in the Bible, but I had justified myself for so long that I had convinced myself that it was really just a strong suggestion. Something we could write off as based on New Testament culture—as we've done with covering our heads during prayer. Something I could take my time (like my whole life) getting around to. I had decided it wasn't that big a deal as long as I was doing most of the other things God was asking me to do. But through two Scriptures He revealed His truth to me. In John 14:15 He said, "If you love me, you will obey what I command." If I loved Him, I would obey what He has commanded—not just some of it, not just those commands I liked or decided were important for me, but all of them. Being submissive to my husband was actually an act of obedience to Jesus.

God continued to clarify this truth to me by showing me four little words in Scripture that somehow I had missed before. These four little words are found in Ephesians 5:22, which says, "Wives, submit to your husbands *as to the Lord*" (emphasis added). There it was, bright as day: "as to the Lord." I am to submit to my husband in the same way I submit to my Lord. My relationship with Jim is the earthly relationship in which I am to show through my actions how I would treat Jesus Himself. My relationship with Jim is a reflection of how I submit to Christ. My submission to Jim is a command, and as I obey this command I demonstrate my love for Jesus and my willingness to follow Him, whatever He asks me to do.

How wrong I had been. I'd tried to keep these two relationships separate. I'd convinced myself that I could rebel against my husband and not help him to be the best he could possibly be, but still be growing spiritually and obeying God. I was choosing which of God's commands I would obey. And that little one about submission was not on my obey list. Surely God would overlook that one oversight on my part. It couldn't be that big a deal, could it?

Sin is sin. It must be confessed and repented of in order to restore our relationship with God. I could no longer fool myself that everything was okay between God and me. My heart was hurting and the conviction was strong. I dropped to my knees and confessed my sin of rebellion against both Jesus and Jim. As I cried, I realized how I wanted to show Jesus how much I loved Him, and as I did, He showed me how to do that. Out of all our relationships here on earth, our relationship with our husband is unique. The most important uniqueness is that this is the only relationship that allows us to show Christ how much we love Him through our submission. We're not commanded to submit to anyone else here on earth "as to the Lord." Although we can show our love for Christ in how we love and care for each other, it is through our submission to our husbands that we give Christ the gift of our submission to Him as well.

**IT'S TIME TO EVALUATE YOURSELF**

Just as in the last two chapters, it is now time to consider how well you're doing. Are you doing your job as wife to the best of your ability?

As in the previous chapters, I encourage you to spend a few minutes in prayer, seeking God and asking Him to open your eyes to how you're doing. Tell Him you want to obey His commands and surrender your headstrong nature. Tell Him you're willing to see yourself as He sees you. Then go through the section below, rating yourself on how well you are currently doing in each category. Many of us strong-willed wives have an unrelenting desire for perfection. As you read through the following evaluation, keep in mind that all wives have areas where we can grow. Use this as a measuring stick to reveal where you need the most improvement. You may want to come back to it again after you've worked on these skills for a while and evaluate how much you have grown. (More on how to work on your behavior in chapter 14 and following.)

Here's a challenge if you are brave and would like feedback to help you grow in your role as a wife. Make a copy of this evaluation and give it to your husband. Ask him to give you feedback on where you are doing well and where you still need to improve.

## My Personal Job Performance Evaluation

Take time to prayerfully rate yourself on each
of the following categories.

### I Act as a Help Meet to My Husband

| 1 | 2 | 3 | 4 | 5 |
|---|---|---|---|---|
| Never | | Sometimes | | Almost Always |

## I Show Respect to My Husband

| 1 | 2 | 3 | 4 | 5 |
|---|---|---|---|---|
| Never | | Sometimes | | Almost Always |

## I Am Submissive to My Husband

| 1 | 2 | 3 | 4 | 5 |
|---|---|---|---|---|
| Never | | Sometimes | | Almost Always |

**COMING UP NEXT**

This chapter may have been difficult for you. I wouldn't be surprised if you seriously considered throwing this book across the room about the time that dirty "s" word showed up. If you're strong willed, you probably feel you already know what that word means, and you don't like it. Let me suggest that there's a tiny possibility that you don't know what it means. Myths about submission abound, and the myths—not the reality—may be what send you running away screaming. So before we get into what the Bible does say, let's clear away some of what it doesn't say.

# CHAPTER 11

# The Myths About Submission

I ONCE SAW A cartoon of a pastor standing up to preach behind a metal wall that surrounded the platform. As he peeked through a small hole to view his congregation, he began, "Our subject today is biblical submission." As I begin this chapter, I feel much like that pastor. I'd better have some protection in place as I discuss this topic, because the opposition usually starts as soon as the word is spoken. So I find myself praying harder than usual for the right words.

Misconceptions regarding submission abound. Many women cringe at the thought that any modern, intelligent, educated, and career-oriented woman would even suggest that God calls wives to be submissive to their husbands. "Isn't that outdated?" I don't believe any of God's commandments ever become outdated. Although society has moved away from God's original plan for marriage, I don't believe God has moved one inch. He is the creator of marriage and therefore knows best how it works.

I believe we women have become resistant to the idea of submission. We do want to obey God, but we don't understand what God meant, so we have become victims of inappropriate applications of this concept. I hope to dispel at least a few of the misconceptions and show how God's original plan for marriage is healthy and honors everyone involved.

## MYTH 1: "IF I AM SUBMISSIVE, I WILL LOSE MY IDENTITY AND HAVE TO DO WHATEVER MY HUSBAND TELLS ME TO DO."

Society says if we are submissive we will lose part or all of who we are, become doormats and be taken advantage of, and become slaves who are forced to serve as our husbands' yes-women. The belief seems to be that if you choose to be submissive it means you have to:

- do what your husband does.
- believe what your husband believes.
- like what your husband likes.
- go where your husband goes.
- say what your husband says or tells you to say.
- and on and on.

But biblical submission does *not* require you to be a doormat or a slave. It does not mean that your personality, abilities, talents, or individuality are buried or lost. It does not mean that your brain will turn to mush and you will no longer have an intelligent thing to say. Submission does not take away who you are, but rather it allows you to develop your God-given potential to its fullest under your husband's encouragement and protection.

I challenge you while you're striving to be more submissive, to search out who God created you to be. He made you unique with gifts that are to be used for His glory. He doesn't want those to go to waste while you turn yourself into a clone of your husband. If He needed another one of your husband, He would have created one. But He didn't. He created you, and He wants you to be just what He planned for you.

Nor does biblical submission mean doing whatever your husband tells you to do. It does not involve blind obedience, total passivity, or a dictator-type ruler. Actually, the word *obedience* implies "have to." The person is required to do whatever is being asked or there will be a consequence. However, the word *submission* means "choose to." Biblical submission can only occur when the person submitting has the choice to submit or not, to do her own thing or what is being requested of her. It cannot be required or forced upon you. In the next chapter you will learn more specifically how a wife can have a heart of submission and yet be able to say no to her husband's requests. As we learn more about what submission truly is, we will dispel the myth of blind obedience and learn how we can remain our own person and still honor God and obey His commands.

## MYTH 2: "SUBMITTING MEANS ACCEPTING THAT I AM INFERIOR."

The thought that submission means "inferior" is one of the biggest reasons I hear from women fighting against it. But submission does not imply that women are inferior to men! It in no way says we are less capable, less valuable, less intelligent, weaker, or second-class citizens. Submission relates to establishing order. Much like the hierarchy or chain of command in any well-working military, government, or business, the family must have some order if it is to run smoothly. This doesn't suggest that those at the top of the chain of command are more valuable than those further down. As a matter of fact, in many companies those at the top of the ladder are most expendable with the least impact on the company's actual workings. So if value is defined as being "necessary to the functioning of," then maybe those toward the bottom are actually the most valuable. My point is, submission does not assign value or importance. It simply assigns rank order or a chain of command.

Husband and wife are of equal importance, but they have been assigned different roles. Like a lock and key, these different roles cannot operate efficiently without the other. And like the president and vice president of a company, the chain of command helps things run as smoothly as possible. The roles are defined for each position, but each is still vital to the working of the whole. They work together toward the same goal but perform different tasks. The president can and should delegate to the vice president what is appropriate, knowing that the vice president is totally capable of managing that task. However, the president is still ultimately responsible for the workings of the company.

Men and women are equal in God's eyes (see Galatians 3:26-29). However, equal does not mean that there are no differences. Spiritually we are equal, but functionally we are different. Different does not imply deficient. You can have two items that are totally equal in weight (one pound of sugar and one pound of coffee beans) but completely different in characteristics and uses. Does that make one of them more valuable than the other? Does it mean that one of them has something wrong with it or is inferior to the other? Of course not! Because of our differences, we as a couple, family, church, and society can accomplish much. If we were all alike—with all the exact same traits, thoughts, and abilities—how much would get accomplished?

Consider a football team full of only quarterbacks, running backs, or kickers. How close would they get to the ultimate goal of a Super Bowl ring? They'd have a hard time getting through even the first game.

On any type of team, all skills are necessary if the ultimate prize is to be won. The quarterback is no more valuable than any other player. But because there needs to be order, he is responsible for calling the plays on the field. The other team members follow the play he called, not because they have to, but because they all have the same ultimate goal: to win. If each player decided to run his own play, it would be chaos!

The body of Christ has many different parts, but all are of equal importance. Paul said God designed us this way "so that there should be no division in the body, but that its parts should have equal concern for each other. If one part suffers, every part suffers with it; if one part is honored, every part rejoices with it" (1 Corinthians 12:25-26).

## MYTH 3: "TRUE SUBMISSION MEANS GIVING UP MY CAREER AND STAYING HOME WITH THE KIDS."

Submission does not mean that you can't be active outside the home. It is not wrong to have a professional career. God did not give you talents and then tell you not to use them.

This is one of the myths that I personally have believed. I haven't let myself admit it out loud, but a part of me believed true Christian women, who were really serving God and submitting to their husbands, were the ones who stayed at home and took care of the kids. A part of me held on to the lie that I wasn't as good or spiritual as my friends who stayed home full-time with their kids. I used to laughingly say, "God just didn't make me to be a stay-at-home mom," while secretly wondering, *Why not? What's wrong with me?*

Eventually I became aware that I was holding two completely opposite beliefs. On one hand, I believed God called me to be a Christian psychologist, a role that required me to work outside the home. On the other hand, I believed that obedience to His command to be submissive meant I needed to be at home with the kids. I avoided Scriptures and sermons that addressed submission, because I couldn't reconcile these opposing forces. These two beliefs were so contrary that I had to choose which one to believe and then attempt to justify or ignore the other. I finally did that by deciding God didn't make me like those other women and I would have to make the best of it. But I kept an underlying feeling of inferiority.

Working on this book helped me realize that I'd held on to this misconception. God revealed His truth to me through a very wise man, my husband. I was reading everything I could get my hands on about submission. I'd read a lot, and as I did, an awful feeling in the pit of my stomach kept getting worse. I tried to push it away. I kept telling myself to stay logical—after all, I was just reading for information. But as I kept reading, the same thing kept standing out, a flashing neon sign: "Godly, submissive women put their husbands and children before themselves. They manage the home. They do not seek after a career of their own." And then there I was, a crying, blubbering mess of a woman saying horrible things to myself.

I decided something had to change. How could I write a book about biblical submission and reject one essential of submission: being a homemaker? I calmed down just enough to dial the phone and waited for my husband to answer. As soon as he did, the tears gushed again, catching Jim off guard and making him wonder what had happened to put me into hysterics. Between gasps I eventually got out what I was trying to say: "I just wanted you to know that I'm going to have to quit my job."

Needless to say, Jim was shocked and confused. I explained what I had been reading and how everything seemed to be saying that I was not being submissive as long as I was working outside the home. Without skipping a beat, his godly wisdom came through. He asked me to define submission. I told him that I thought it meant being willing to do what my leader asked me to do, even if it wasn't what I wanted. Then he asked me who I was to be submissive to. That was easy, "you and God." And then I heard the words that freed me from a bondage that I hadn't even realized I was under: "Did God or I ask you to be a stay-at-home mom?" A quiet "no" was my only response.

He continued, "If God and I aren't asking that of you, then how are you not being submissive? You told me you felt called into this ministry long before we ever decided to get married. I knew that when I married you, and I committed my life to you knowing you'd be serving God on a full-time basis outside our home. I'm just thankful to be serving Him right beside you."

Wow! I had never seen it that way. I wasn't being rebellious to my husband, because my husband had never asked me to stay at home. I was doing what both God and my husband wanted me to do. There's no rebellion in that. The guilt I'd felt all that time and anew from well-meaning Christian teachers was not from being disobedient, but rather from holding on to a false belief that is constantly presented.

Submission is not about any specific behaviors you are or are not to engage in. It's not about a set of rules that someone else places on you. And it's definitely not an all-or-nothing concept. It's true, aspects of my attitude needed to change in my relationship to Jim to allow my submissive heart to take over. But that didn't mean that all my behaviors had to change. I didn't have to quit my job to have a submissive heart. Submission is about knowing what God (first) and your husband (second) request from you and then doing your best to fulfill those requests out of love. It's about understanding the goals of your marital team and then using your specific talents to help your team reach those goals. It doesn't mean you can't have a career. Instead, it means that your career doesn't take over and become your number one priority at the expense of your relationship with God, your husband, or your family. I know this can be a delicate balancing act, but as long as you keep the order in place, God can bless you as you evaluate and accomplish your endeavors.

## MYTH 4: "GOD ONLY EXPECTS ME TO BE SUBMISSIVE AS LONG AS MY HUSBAND TREATS ME RIGHT."

I have heard this and similar statements from many women. There seems to be a mass belief that submission is something that our husbands earn as a reward for good behavior. Once they learn to treat us with the love and respect we deserve, then we just might show a little submissiveness to them—but even then, only if it serves our purposes.

However, God doesn't give a command and then give a list of exceptions to the rule. Did God say any of this?

"Wives, submit to your husbands as long as he is

- Right
- Christlike

- Nice
- Gentle
- Lovable
- Respectful
- Honoring
- Loving . . .

Otherwise, feel free to skip this command."

Just as we would not take one of the Ten Commandments and decide when we'll obey it, we cannot decide when we will or won't choose to be submissive. Submission is a command and is therefore expected from us all the time, not just when our husband has earned it or we feel like giving it. Submission is not something we can hold back until our husband decides to start loving us as he's supposed to.

Peter said a wife should submit even to a non-Christian husband: "Wives, in the same way be submissive to your husbands so that, if any of them do not believe the word, they may be won over without words by the behavior of their wives, when they see the purity and reverence of your lives" (1 Peter 3:1-2). Even when it seems logical that we might not need to be submissive, Peter says we should do so anyway. There are no exceptions to our submission unless our husband asks us to do something that is contrary to the Word of God.

## MYTH 5: "SUBMISSION MEANS I WILL HAVE TO ENDURE ABUSE."

On the other hand, this myth goes to the opposite extreme. It's possibly the scariest and most destructive of the myths. Women have told me they are remaining in an abusive relationship "because God told me to" or "because the Bible says

I am to submit to him no matter what." I heard this one and wanted to cry: "My pastor told me to go home and be more submissive. He said that if I just serve my husband better and stop arguing with him, then things will get better."

This is nonsense! The Bible does not say it is okay to participate in or knowingly allow a sinful behavior as long as we can prove that it was forced upon us. Even 1 Peter 2-3, which is commonly pointed to justify enduring abuse, indicates submission as to the Lord. As a matter of fact, Scripture tells us to flee from sinful activities (see 1 Timothy 6:11). Abuse is sin, and God does not condone sin! God did not command submission as a way of justifying a man's treating his wife inappropriately, nor as a reason for her to stay with an abusive man.

Although Jesus wasn't married to an abusive spouse, He did experience people whose anger got out of control. Let's look at how Jesus responded to anger that was out of control and harmful. Luke tells of a time when Jesus was visiting his hometown of Nazareth. When the Sabbath came, He went to the synagogue and read from the Old Testament scrolls. As He talked about the passage from Isaiah, it says, "All the people in the synagogue were furious when they heard this. They got up, drove him out of the town, and took him to the brow of the hill on which the town was built, in order to throw him down the cliff" (Luke 4:28-29). Now I don't know about you, but that sounds like abuse to me. Here's the best part: "But he walked right through the crowd and went on his way" (verse 30). Jesus refused to allow Himself to be abused. He removed Himself from the aggressive people who intended to harm Him. I believe He expects the same from a wife (or anyone, for that matter) who is in danger of being hurt physically, sexually, or emotionally.

As we learned in chapter 10, we are to submit to our husbands "as to the Lord" (Ephesians 5:22). We are to show them the love and respect we would show Jesus. But Jesus would never sin against us, and He would not expect us to remain in a situation where someone else was. He does not condone sin, and neither should we. And abuse, regardless of the type, is sin.

Defining abuse can be difficult, and I'm sure each of us would have a somewhat different description. But I hope we would all agree that abuse refers to more than just the physical abuse we think of first. Of course hitting is wrong and should never be tolerated. But there are so many other ways of abusing your spouse than just hitting him or her. Even physical abuse includes more than just hitting. What about pushing and shoving? Physically holding a person against her will? Inappropriate or unwanted sexual contact? These are all physical abuse.

But we must also consider emotional, mental, and psychological abuse as wrong and intolerable. Should people have to endure name calling? Intimidation? Fits of rage that "come close" but never make physical impact? Mind games that make them doubt themselves? Adultery? I believe the list could go on and on. When we treat our spouse as Christ would treat him or her, none of these abuses will ever be present, and none should be tolerated. We need to examine ourselves here as well.

I am not saying that none of us will ever be hurt or persecuted for the sake of Christ. But that is not what we are talking about here. Domestic violence is about power and dominance—not about Christ—and should be stopped. If you are in an abusive relationship, I strongly encourage you to seek immediate help in dealing with this situation. I recommend that you seek counsel from a respected Christian therapist who can guide you to the best way to stop the abuse. This may include: each of you getting counseling to work through how to better manage your anger; the two of you together attending marriage counseling to change the pattern of interactions between you; or even having a "constructive separation" that allows you to be protected by removing yourself from the situation, while you then seek counsel to work on the possibility of reunifying the relationship once it's healthier and safer for all involved.

## MYTH 6: "IF I'M A SUBMISSIVE WIFE I WILL MAKE NO DECISIONS AND EXPRESS NO OPINIONS OR THOUGHTS OF MY OWN."

How much sense does that make? That would be poor stewardship of time and resources. God did not create you as the silent partner of the marriage. He created you to be your husband's helper. You can't be a good helper if you don't share your ideas. God didn't give you a job and then tell you not to do it. And He didn't give you ideas and tell you to keep them to yourself.

A good leader should always delegate in areas where he knows he has someone he can trust to manage well (maybe even better than he could himself). This allows him more freedom and time to manage other areas, so more is accomplished than any one person could do alone.

The Bible gives us a great example of this concept in Proverbs 31. This godly woman was more valuable to her husband than jewels. Let's see if she made decisions and expressed thoughts, and if her husband delegated to her. We are told that:

- "she selects wool and flax" (verse 13)
- "she considers a field and buys it" (verse 16)
- she makes trades and sees that they are profitable (verse 18)
- she seems to run at least a couple of different businesses—a vineyard (verse 16) and garment sales (verse 24)
- she manages both her family and her servants (verses 15,27)
- "she speaks with wisdom, and faithful instruction is on her tongue" (verse 26)

She makes decisions every time she turns around, and she speaks out of her wisdom. Her husband "has full confidence in her" (verse 11) and "praises her" (verse 28). He is not threatened by her abilities; he encourages her to be all she can be. And he enjoys the benefits of her successes, as indicated in verses 11-12: he "lacks nothing of value," and "she brings him good, not harm." He brings public attention to her accomplishments. He says, "Give her the reward she has earned, and let her works bring her praise at the city gate" (verse 31).

Based on this description of a godly wife, I'd say it's more than appropriate under God's plan for marriage for the wife not only to make some decisions, but to be in charge of the areas of life that she and her husband agree she is well-equipped to handle. In those agreed-upon areas, where a wife has expertise and can make good decisions, the husband should delegate to her and encourage her to manage. This delegating must come with some level of trust and autonomy. She cannot be told this is her area to take charge of and then constantly be questioned, told how she should have done it, or required to check with her husband before making any decisions.

Certainly you discuss the big decisions and the different areas of your lives. You don't do things behind each other's back. That would not be acting as a team. Being a good team means using your God-given skills to best benefit the marriage as a whole and yet always being aware that you are not acting alone. Of course you will inform each other about what you have been doing and what you plan to do next. It is just not required that you check in before every step. You may even have the final say in the areas your husband has delegated to you. You should, however, be willing to hand this back to your husband if it becomes more than you can handle.

Healthy couples have a husband who is secure in himself and a wife who doesn't have to prove herself. In these couples, the husband gives his wife as much responsibility as she's equipped for and willing to accept. A wise husband will help his wife develop her gifts to her fullest potential by delegating to her in the areas where she functions best. He will encourage her to become the best she can be, because that's why God gave her those abilities. Although a husband may keep track of the overall big picture of his family, he's the best steward of his time and resources when he delegates to his wife those things she's equipped to manage.

As we wrap up this chapter, I hope it has dispelled at least a few myths that may have held you back from embracing submission. I believe we strong-willed wives will never become as submissive as God means us to be until we acknowledge our false beliefs about submission. Once we resolve these, our fears of submission will begin to subside.

**COMING UP NEXT**

Now that we have faced some of the horrible ways God's command to submit to our husbands has been twisted, I hope we can see that submission is not something to be feared. Then our strong-willed nature will allow us to accept this concept as fitting into who we really are. We will stop fearing a loss of who we are and instead embrace a more satisfying view of who God created us to be.

## Real Submission

IN CHAPTER 7 YOU met Mark and Isabel, two very strong-willed people. They were initially attracted to each other because of their mutual independence and type-A personality styles. But as time progressed, these same traits pulled them apart. As two young children joined their home and Isabel worked only part-time, they increasingly wondered why they ever married in the first place. They seemed to want such totally different things from life now. Isabel's focus was on the home and family, and Mark's remained on his personal career and hobbies.

Mark and Isabel agreed that before Isabel became pregnant unexpectedly with their first child, they were on the same path. They were both career driven and enjoyed their financial and personal freedom. But nothing was the same after the birth of their son. Finances were tight, couple time was in short supply, and sex was on the verge of extinction. Although they had not planned on having children yet, it had happened, and as a result, Isabel's focus moved from enhancing her career to expanding her family. Their son was barely eight months old when she started talking about having another baby.

Mark couldn't believe it. Not so long before they had seriously considered never having kids, and now here she was ready to have more. He wasn't anywhere close to being ready for that and was very vocal in saying so. He didn't like what parenthood was doing to his relationship with his wife. She never seemed to have time for him, they never went out as a couple anymore, and she was too tired to have sex. They seemed to be growing further and further apart.

Mark threw himself even more into his career with the excuse that he had to make up for the loss of income when Isabel moved to part-time work. But they both knew that was only part of the reason. Isabel felt more and more lonely and believed another baby would bring them back together. Mark was good with their son, when he was around, and she thought another child would encourage him to be home more. She knew Mark said he wanted to wait, but she thought if it "just happened" again, he would be thrilled.

As a result of her plans, their sexual relationship improved drastically over the next few months. Mark thought things were turning around and life might get back to normal. But he was soon hit with a bombshell. Baby number two was on the way.

This pattern of self-centeredness had plagued their marriage from the beginning, but this was the ultimate blow. Instead of growing closer, the wedge of distance between Mark and Isabel was driven deeper. They were living separate lives under the same roof. Isabel was miserable and searched for something to turn things around. She got back into her Bible study and joined a women's group at church that was focused on "being all you can be for God." That sounded like just what she needed. She wanted to get her priorities right again and start putting God first. She was sure that was all she needed.

After several weeks of various topics in her women's group, eventually the topic turned to marriage and "being all you can be as a Christian wife." She almost decided to skip that one, because she was sure her marriage was a lost cause. She sure didn't want to hear a lecture on being submissive. But she went and was pleasantly surprised. Yes, the topic of submission came up but in a different way than she had ever heard before.

The leader talked about the marriage covenant and how the vows we take are designed to keep us other-focused instead of self-focused. We commit to love the other no matter what, and our goal in marriage is to become one flesh. There is no room for selfishness within the oneness of marriage. The leader said the intimacy that couples strive for comes from the letting go of self and joining together to achieve a mutual goal of a forever marriage. And she said that submission to our husbands is actually submission to that mutually taken vow to love each other "in sickness and health, for richer or poorer. . . ." Submission is the process of putting off our selfish desires and putting on "one flesh." It isn't about doing what the husband says no matter what, but about doing those things that are necessary to reach the ultimate goal of a God-honoring marriage that will last forever.

Isabel left that meeting with hope. She knew that she had not put her vows or the marriage relationship as her top priority, because she had always kept her personal desires as number one. She knew that she had not been submissive, because she didn't know what it really meant. And what she thought it meant, although false, was scary enough to her that she avoided it at all cost. Her fresh understanding made her realize that she had to stop focusing on herself if she wanted a healthy marriage. She was ready to confess this to Mark and to start making changes. She was nervous about his reaction but excited about the possibilities for their future if they worked on this together.

## GETTING TO THE TRUTH

We spent the last chapter dispelling myths associated with submission. But if submission is not all of those things, then what is it?

What's left after you remove the negative ideas is what I believe God truly intended for us to understand about submission. He never intended submission to put women down and keep them in "their place." He never wanted women to feel inferior to men or less valuable to Him. He wanted submission to bring about oneness between husband and wife. But as the Enemy is so quick to do, he twisted this command into something degrading to women. Then it didn't take much to get women fighting against it.

As long as we hold on to Satan's lies, he'll continue to win and marriages will continue to be destroyed. It's time that we dig into Scripture, pour ourselves into prayer, and earnestly seek God to reveal to each of us what He intended.

## WHERE DID SUBMISSION BEGIN?

Although Ephesians 5 is the most often quoted section of Scripture regarding submission, it is not where submission began. It began with God Himself. Before there was anything, there was God. We speak of God as a Holy Trinity, because He is three distinct Persons—God the Father, God the Son, and God the Holy Spirit—yet undivided in His essence. The Three are united as One God and yet distinct. It's within this Holy Trinity of God that submission has its root. And I believe it is the Trinity itself that gives us the key to what submission is to be.

The word *Trinity* means "three in one." The Three serve different roles but do not represent different levels of importance. The members of the Trinity are a team working together to accomplish the same ultimate goals. One of God's goals has been the creation of and later the redemption of humanity. Each member of the Trinity has a different job to accomplish that ultimate goal. And it is the Trinity's oneness that makes it all possible.

To accomplish this goal, God planned leadership and order, and therefore submission, within the Trinity. Paul explains this: "Now I want you to realize that the head of every man is Christ, and the head of the woman is man, and the head of Christ is God" (1 Corinthians 11:3). Jesus said that He always did the will of the Father and was subject to Him (see John 6:38).

We can see order and submission when we look at relationships within the Trinity. God the Father sent the Son, who submitted and obeyed the Father's will even to death to gain our salvation. The Son then sent the Holy Spirit to continue His work here on earth and to serve as our Comforter. Here we see the uniqueness of God's roles but the oneness of His purpose, all Three working together toward the same end.

Further, consider what Paul said about Jesus in Philippians:

Who, being in very nature God,
[Jesus] did not consider equality with God
something to be grasped,
but made himself nothing,

taking the very nature of a servant,
being made in human likeness.
And being found in appearance as a man,
he humbled himself
and became obedient to death —
even death on a cross!
(Philippians 2:6-8)

Jesus prayed, "not my will, but yours" (Luke 22:42), and was submissive even unto death. If God Himself models submission, how much more should we follow His example? It's never wrong to follow the example that Christ Himself gave us — we're to be followers and imitators of Christ. But does that mean even on the submissive thing? Absolutely!

## A NEED FOR ORDER

So many voices in our society work to convince us that submission is wrong or outdated. Believing what society says about submission is easier and more comfortable than believing what God says. I agree that the term has been misused, misunderstood, and misapplied. But submission as it is described in Scripture is not wrong. Just because a God-given command has been wrongly used and misunderstood does not give us the right to forget the whole thing and reject it. We must learn what God meant and start applying it in that context to our marriages, or the trend of destruction will continue.

I believe that one major cause of the breakdown of our families is our ignorance of, and our unwillingness to apply, God's concept of submission. Society has pushed women to step in and take over in almost every area of life. As we choose to respond to this pressure, we also choose to step out from under God's provision. Thus, if we are honest, we strong-willed wives hold at least some responsibility for undermining our marriages.

Homes need order, and order involves leadership. But even more than that, marriages need oneness between husband and wife. If we handle the issue of becoming one as husband and wife and address the selfishness of our current world, I believe the issue of leadership and submission will completely change. When we can blend instead of separate, and when we can work toward the same ultimate goals instead of toward our own selfish desires, then the issue of order within marriage will likely become a non-issue altogether. We will be comfortable using our God-given strengths to move the marriage forward as one unit, not as two individuals. We will accept God's ordained order within the family, because we will see it as the means of achieving our ultimate goal of oneness.

Even as order and leadership were essential for oneness within the Holy Trinity, so it is for marriage. God gave that position of leadership to the husband. But in the last few decades, we've stood by and watched as society has organized a mutiny in marriages and women have overthrown God's ordained leader. Men have abdicated their God-given responsibilities to verbally aggressive, competitive wives, and those who haven't have been ridiculed and called "chauvinistic pigs" (or maybe even worse).

Books upon books upon books have been written in these last few decades on how to help this husband who has just been overthrown learn to understand and live peaceably with his new-generation wife and how to change himself to better relate to the woman of today. Other books give the wife suggestions on how to get her husband to better meet her needs and serve her. Now don't get me wrong, I'm not saying many of these changes weren't needed. It didn't hurt most men to make a few adjustments, as it wouldn't hurt most of us. However, the societal trend has focused on getting men to make changes with minimal focus on what we wives could do to improve our marriages. Even our focus on how to change has been separate and one-sided. In order for marriages to heal, we have to stop focusing on our separateness and start learning how to become one. We need to learn how to work toward the same ultimate goal of a God-honoring marriage that will last "until death us do part."

**FROM THE BEGINNING OF HUMAN EXISTENCE**

Not only was order and submission necessary within the Godhead, it was also needed at the beginning of life on earth. God created humans male and female—equal but different. They had different roles and responsibilities, not different value to God or each other. In order to establish leadership and order, He told the woman, "Your desire will be for your husband, and he will rule over you" (Genesis 3:16). This was not a definition of her value or her abilities, but of authority structure. And before the Fall,

> God created man in his own image,
> in the image of God he created him;
> male and female he created them. (Genesis 1:27)

God created them different but did not make one less of a person than the other. He filled them each with different aspects of Himself. He created them male and female—both in His image. Not man in God's image and woman as an afterthought with the leftovers.

Creating woman was God's statement that creation and His image were not complete without her. Although Adam had everything a man could want—a perfect home, an interesting job, and fellowship with God—he still had a void, loneliness. God knew from the beginning that this would not be good, and He had a plan in place to complete both man and the image of God. His plan was woman, a "helper suitable for him" and the completeness of the image of God. That's what we are as women, the completeness of the image of God. When joined as one, the husband and wife together reflect the image of our heavenly Father. But within that oneness of marriage, there must be order. There still must be leadership and submission.

## WHAT SUBMISSION REALLY IS

Now that we've figured out what submission is not and where it developed from, let's see what it is. I'm not a Greek or Hebrew scholar or even a theologian, so I won't go deeply into the definition of the words other than what you could find in a good concordance. I will focus, however, on defining the concept of submission by using Scripture and the model Christ left for us through His life and actions here on earth.

### Submission Is Voluntary
*Submission* can be contrasted with *obedience*. Obedience is something that a person in authority requires from his subordinates. There is no choice. In fact, obedience is usually used to describe situations where a negative consequence results when the subject does not do what is required of him.

We often require our children's obedience regardless of what they may personally want. Doing what someone asks you to do when there is really no other choice is not categorized as submission, but rather obedience or compliance.

For a person to be truly submissive, they must have a choice whether or not to be so. The person in authority requests something, but the subordinate knows she can comply or not. In order to meet the true biblical meaning of the word, submission must be freely and willingly given. Your husband cannot require this of you; he cannot force it upon you or threaten you into doing it. (So, strong-willed women, set your minds at ease.) That would not be biblical submission. That would be complying out of fear of retaliation, and that type of fear is not from God. And, although God has assigned you this submissive role, even He doesn't force you to take it any more than He forced His Son, Jesus, to die on the cross.

Jesus knew it was God's will that He come to earth, live a sinless life, die on the cross, and be raised again on the third day in order to purchase our salvation. This was God's will, but Jesus had a choice. Yet because God the Father and God the Son were of the same mind and were striving for the same goal, Jesus submitted and did the Father's will. Even before His betrayal, Jesus knew what was coming and openly expressed Himself to the Father. He asked (pleaded really) for this cup to pass from Him. But He immediately followed that with "not my will, but yours be done" (Luke 22:42).

Jesus was God, and He could have chosen to walk away from that task. Walking away wouldn't have caused any consequences for Him (although it would have been devastating for us). He still would have been God. But being submissive also would not cause Him to lose who He was. He

didn't have to stop being God in order to submit and die on
the cross. And we as wives do not have to lose who we have
been created to be when we choose to submit.

We see that it was Christ's submission to the Father that
brought Him glory and honor. Again we look at Philippians 2:

And being found in appearance as a man,
    he humbled himself
    and became obedient to death —
    even death on a cross!
Therefore God exalted him to the highest place
    and gave him the name that is above every name,
that at the name of Jesus every knee should bow,
    in heaven and on earth and under the earth,
and every tongue confess that Jesus Christ is Lord,
    to the glory of God the Father.
    (Philippians 2:8-11)

Now do you think submission devalues you?

*Submission Is a Spiritual Measuring Stick for Wives*
Remember in chapter 10 when we discussed that we are to
submit to our husbands "as to the Lord"? If you don't get
anything else out of this book, please get this! As much as we
strong-willed wives struggle in the very depths of who we are
with this submission thing, it all boils down to this: The way
we treat our husbands here on earth is a direct reflection of
how we are doing spiritually. It is the one and only relationship we have that God is looking at as a mirror image of how
we would treat Him if He were standing among us. I know
we find that hard to swallow. Each of us knows in our hearts
that if Christ were sitting in our living room in the flesh, we

would treat Him like the King He is. But would we?

God has given us the perfect opportunity to show Him how much we love Him. He gave us a husband to love, respect, and submit to just as we would submit to Him if He were sitting beside us. He wants to see our love for Him through the way we love and treat our husbands each day of our lives. He's using our relationship with our husband as a measuring stick as to how much we really, truly love Him.

Do you love your Savior? Do you really love Him? Do you love Him enough to obey all of His commands to you? Do you love Him enough to be submissive to your husband?

*Submission Is More of an Attitude Than an Action*

You may have heard the story of the small boy who, upon being disobedient to his parent, was sent directly to his time-out chair. He went to where the chair was but refused to sit in it. His mother sternly "helped" him sit only to watch him stand up again with his arms tightly crossed. After repeating this interaction a couple of times, the mother's patience wore thin and she explained the further consequences for this young man if he refused to sit in the chair. With an angry huff, the little boy plopped his bottom into the chair. As the mother walked away she heard, "I may be sitting on the outside, but I'm standing on the inside!"

Does this sound like you? Are you going through the actions that make it appear as if you are being submissive to your husband, but harboring anger and resentments internally? Or are you secretly hoping to manipulate the situation to go your way? Or maybe you are expecting God to step in and make it right (as defined by you)?

The requirements of biblical submission can only be met by a willing heart. Biblical submission is freely yielding your own will to the will of another, no strings attached. There can be no self-serving motives in your submission. If you submit with expectations and these expectations are not met, then resentment may develop. Freely giving a part of yourself does not result in resentment. When we feel something is being taken from us or required of us, something we must give when we don't want to, then the negative emotions around submission begin to grow.

If you struggle with feelings of anger or resentment, I suggest that you take some time to evaluate the motives behind your submissive behavior. Are you submitting out of obedience to Christ and respect for your husband? Or are you more concerned with how you look to others or what consequences may come to you (from either your husband or God) if you don't submit?

The motives behind the behavior must be pure and not self-seeking in order to experience the blessings that can come through submitting to Christ and our husbands. Keep this in mind: "All a man's ways seem right to him, but the LORD weighs the heart" (Proverbs 21:2), and "The LORD does not look at the things man looks at. Man looks at the outward appearance, but the LORD looks at the heart" (1 Samuel 16:7). Submission is to be done "as to the Lord," so be sure that what the Lord sees is a willing heart.

*Submission Can Involve Disagreement*
So is it really possible to be submissive and still disagree with your husband? Can you ever say no to him without feeling guilty that you have committed some grievous sin? Of course. But to reach this point, understand that submission is about doing what must be done to achieve the mutual goal and commitment between the two of you. On your wedding

day you joined together in a covenant before God and man to become one flesh. You both stated your desire to have a marriage that lasted "until death us do part." You both must be willing to set aside your selfish desires to accomplish that covenant. And therefore, if your husband requests behaviors of you that go against the fulfillment of that covenant, you may find yourself saying no to him and yet submitting to a God-honoring marriage.

For example, when Isabel went home and talked to Mark about what she had learned at her women's group and about her desire to make some changes to improve their marriage, Mark was thrilled. All he could think about was how this meant he would finally get what he needed from this marriage. Isabel would start being submissive! He thought he'd never see the day. Isabel was surprised by Mark's reaction and wasn't exactly sure why he was being so pleasant about it, but she wasn't going to complain.

Over the next couple of weeks things went well between them. They talked more without arguing—partly because she was choosing her battles more carefully. Whereas in the past she argued or complained about almost everything Mark did, she now thought about whether or not his requests were things that would hurt the marriage. If she decided they would not, she accepted his choices more easily. Her focus had changed, and she felt good about being less selfish in her reactions. And she was realizing that he wasn't doing as much wrong as she had thought. She saw more positives in him and told him so.

When he said he was planning to play golf on Saturday, she used to see that as avoiding family time. But now she saw that he needed some "self-time" after a stressful week at work and actually encouraged him to go. The best part of this was that he came home from the golf course and actually seemed happy to be home. He played with the kids and helped fix dinner without her asking.

She thought everything was going great until one evening Mark announced that he was purchasing a new computer. A friend at work got a great deal on the most up-to-date laptop, and now Mark wanted one too. Isabel reacted without thinking—just as she had in the past when Mark made a big purchase: "Are you crazy?! There's no way we can afford a laptop. We're barely paying our bills now!"

Mark retorted, "Who are you to tell me what I can do with *my* money? And besides, I thought you were working on being submissive! You don't sound submissive now."

Isabel was cut deeply by his comments and left the room. She felt badly about the way she had responded, but she also knew they really couldn't afford this purchase. She had just paid bills that morning, and they had a whole $150 in the bank. She knew unwise past purchases got them to this place, and if they were ever going to pull themselves out of it, they both had to stop spending money they didn't have. And they had agreed together on that not long ago.

But she wasn't sure how the whole submission thing applied here. Was she supposed to submit even to Mark's unwise decisions? Was she supposed to just stand by and let this continue, knowing where they were headed financially? Was she supposed to agree when he said, "Let's not spend anything unnecessarily," and then also agree when he decided he wanted to spend again? It just didn't make sense.

She prayed for wisdom and tried to remember everything she'd been learning about godly submission. She knew this decision would not benefit the marriage and actually would harm them financially. She knew he hadn't made this decision out of their oneness but out of his selfishness. And she knew that spending beyond their means was not good stewardship of the resources God gave them. So she took a deep breath and went to find Mark, knowing she disagreed with him but planning to do so with a loving attitude this time.

Mark was sitting at the computer looking up information about the new laptop he wanted. Isabel was much calmer and shared her concerns. She reminded him of their earlier agreement to work on getting out of debt and stated her belief that they needed to hold true to that decision. She also needed to talk about his response of "you don't sound submissive now." She explained that she believed God didn't intend her to submit to something destructive to the marriage, which she had committed to before Him and planned to be a part of for the rest of her life. That took Mark aback, and he sat silent for several minutes. He had just heard her say she planned to be married for the rest of her life. He hadn't heard that from her in years, and he was letting it soak in. If that was really the case, then maybe he needed to make some changes in his perspective as well. He knew then he didn't need a laptop, he needed his wife! And he would do whatever he had to do to restore this marriage.

**COMING UP NEXT**

We've spent the last couple of chapters working to dispel misconceptions about submission and to alleviate fears we may have about it. In this chapter we have looked at what submission really is once all the baggage is dropped. Simply stated:

**Submission is an attitude of the heart
that says we want to show our love for Christ
through the way we voluntarily place
the goal of oneness within the marriage
before our own selfish desires.**

Now that doesn't look so scary anymore, does it? We love our Savior with everything in us and want everyone to know it. And we're willing to give when giving is working toward a mutual goal and is done under our own free will, not forced. When we submit in this way, we will not feel resentment. We will not feel used or taken advantage of. We will not feel scared or devalued. We will not feel we must do everything we are told to do. We will submit as a way to show how much we love our Savior and our husband, and we will do whatever is necessary to maintain a marriage that will last a lifetime!

So what's stopping us now? Why do we struggle to let go and let God have control of our marriage? In the next chapter we will identify several of the excuses we make as to why we shouldn't or can't submit, and we will acknowledge the fears that we have deep inside that cause us to want to remain in control.

# CHAPTER 13

# Why Won't I Let Him Lead?

WE ARE ALL EXPERTS at making excuses for our behavior. This is no different in leadership or submission. Let's look at three of the most common excuses wives make for not submitting.

## EXCUSE 1: "MY HUSBAND IS JUST NOT THE LEADER TYPE."

Angela sat in my counseling office explaining her marital frustrations. "I'm so tired of acting as the man of the house! I don't think Brent has made a serious decision in our home in our whole thirteen years of marriage. He even asks me to pick out his clothes, because he says I'm better at it than he is. But I think he's just too lazy to do it himself.

"I know I'm strong and a quick decision maker, but even when I ask him to help me with a decision, he won't. He's not mean about it, he just says, 'Whatever you decide will be fine with me.' Well I'm sick of making all the decisions. I'm tired of feeling like I have the weight of the world on my shoulders. But if I don't take care of everything, it simply won't get done.

"I try to back off, thinking he will eventually realize he has to do something, but he doesn't. Last summer I went to a convention for work and was gone for a whole week. You know what he did? Nothing! The house was a mess, the bills I left stamped and ready to be mailed were still sitting there because he 'wasn't sure what day they were supposed to go out.' So instead of asking or just mailing them anyway, he did nothing! I wouldn't be surprised if he went to work in his pajamas, because I wasn't there to pick out his clothes. I feel more like his mother than his wife. I'm so glad we never had children, because I would be responsible for them all by myself too.

"Sunday at church the pastor was talking about being submissive within your marriage, and all I could think about was, *I'd love to submit to my husband if he'd ever give me something to submit to.* He never directly asks me to do anything; he just doesn't do whatever it is, so I have to. He never tells me what he'd like me to do for him. He just says he's happy the way we are. Well, I'm not! How do you make someone be the leader of the home if he doesn't want to be?"

Unfortunately, Angela is not alone. This is probably the number one excuse women give about why they are the leaders in their homes: "He just won't lead. It takes him forever to make even a simple decision. If he won't, then I guess I have to." When I meet these women, my first question is usually something like, "Have you ever let him try?" I start here because many of the husbands I've talked to say, "She won't let me lead." And I know that many strong-willed wives struggle with allowing their husbands to lead even when we say that's what we want. I would say that in about 50 to 60 percent of the cases this is the problem.

As strong-willed wives, we think fast, move fast, and

make decisions fast, and expect others to do the same. What if your husband would be willing to make more decisions but you don't allow him the time he needs to do so? Would you let him even have his choice on a simple negotiable item, if his choice would be different from yours? Husbands who are more passive are often more cautious or slower in making decisions, but that doesn't mean they won't or can't lead. It simply means they don't do it as we would.

Have you given your passive husband the chance he needs to lead? Are you allowing him the time he needs to make the decision? Do you encourage him to make decisions, or do you criticize how long it takes and what he chooses?

If you are married to a passive husband, he will likely continue to be passive as long as you often step in and take over. His natural personality style is comfortable when others are in charge, but that doesn't mean he's not capable. But it is possible that he has become dependent on your leading and therefore doesn't attempt it himself. On the other hand, he may be reluctant to give it a shot out of fear of not meeting your expectations and then suffering your criticism or manipulation.

God didn't command husbands to be the spiritual leaders in their homes and then not equip them to do so. They have the ability within themselves when they rely on God to strengthen them. However, your husband may need to develop this ability with time and practice. You will have to allow him to practice and be patient and encouraging as he does so.

But as I said, this is the problem in a little over half of the cases. What about women like Angela? What happens when you really have tried to back off and allow your husband the opportunity to be the leader, and he still doesn't step up to the plate? What if you are tired of wearing the pants in the family, but he just doesn't want to either? How far are you supposed to go to see if he will take his rightful place as head of the household?

These are tough questions, and there are no easy answers. The basic belief that God doesn't call men to do a job and then not equip them to do it still holds true. The challenge here is, are these men seeking God's strength and provision to help them do their job? The answer is, probably not. And if not, why not?

The reasons these men are not choosing to take their God-given role within the marriage are likely as varied as the men themselves, but they often lie in areas of low self-esteem, feelings of inadequacy, and fear of failure. These all have significant impact on a man's ability to lead his family. These issues need to be dealt with and resolved. The source of these feelings is often deep seated and long-standing, and will best be processed through counseling. If you truly believe that you have backed off and encouraged your husband to take a leadership position within your home, and he has been unable or unwilling to do so, I suggest that you lovingly encourage him to seek a Christian counselor to help him process his resistance to being what God calls him to be and what you need him to be. Once the source of his resistance is identified and he begins to make changes, you will still need to be patient. Family dynamics and personal changes don't happen overnight. A husband who has never led before will need to take on this responsibility in stages, just as you will likely need to release your responsibility and control in stages. As the two of you work on and eventually master each new area, you will establish trust and will be encouraged to take the next step together.

Now let's consider that you are a strong-willed wife married to a strong-willed husband. Can you use the excuse "my husband just isn't the leader type"? Of course. Again, it's not that these men are incapable of leading. It's often more that they have tried for years and years but didn't meet your expectations. Over time they gave up. Even strong-willed husbands reach the point where it's not worth the fight to try to be the leader in a home with a strong-willed wife.

A strong-willed husband told me, "It's just easier to let her do what she's going to do. I stopped trying to give my opinions or persuade her to do it differently long ago. It's just easier to follow her lead than to fight through it." This is a very successful businessman who runs his company and his employees efficiently. So the excuse that he can't or won't lead doesn't fit. He is perfectly capable of doing so, but he has simply decided that within his home he won't. And he's not alone. Many husbands say similar things. Being married to strong-willed wives takes its toll over time, and they stop trying.

Now don't get me wrong, whatever the reason that the husband isn't playing his role doesn't make it right. But it also doesn't justify our excuse to remain in control. We need to bring out the best in our husband just as we hope he brings out the best in us. We need to encourage him to make decisions and take an active role in our home. And we need to let him do it his way. This will build his confidence and motivate him to do more.

**EXCUSE 2: "GOD MUST NOT HAVE KNOWN MY HUSBAND!"**

This was Sharon's second marriage, and she was sure she had chosen better than the first time. At least Craig didn't drink or hit her, but she knew she'd never allow any man to treat her that way again. Still, sometimes she wondered if this was really better. She and Craig had been married ten years and had three beautiful daughters—not that Craig would know. He was so wrapped up in himself and whatever he wanted to do that she wondered if he would even notice if she took the kids and left. She handled everything around the house and managed her own and the girls' lives just fine. Luckily she was strong and able to take care of herself. But that wasn't what she thought marriage was supposed to be like. Why was she married if she felt like a single mom?

The only time she didn't feel invisible to Craig was when he was in the mood for sex. Early in their relationship she almost always gave in to his sexual advances, because it was the only way she could feel close to him. Even when he hadn't been around much or if he had been "playfully" calling her names that made her feel degraded and ugly, she still responded positively when he told her he needed sex. She convinced herself that something was better than nothing and she would take what she could get. Over time she began to use sex to her advantage. She often initiated sex after an argument to smooth things over, because this was better than getting the silent treatment for the next three days.

Because Sharon never said no to Craig sexually, he began to expect more and more from her. Not just in frequency but in the types of sex he "needed." Sometimes she wanted to say "no way," but when she tried, Craig made sarcastic remarks about how he guessed she just didn't really love him. If that didn't work, he made threats about not needing to be married to someone who didn't want to meet his needs. Eventually she always gave in. But she felt dirty afterward and knew this wasn't what God intended their physical relationship to be like.

This pattern took its toll on her, and she gave up trying
to feel connected to Craig. It wasn't worth what it was cost-
ing her. The first few times she said no and meant it, Craig
got furious and left the house for a few hours. But that game
soon ended, and they realized they were at a stalemate.
Neither was moving, and neither was winning. Sharon was
going her own direction and doing her own thing, focusing on
her daughters and living as a roommate with her husband.
She had spent years giving in to Craig, and things only got
worse. If God wanted her to be submissive to her husband
as the pastor was preaching, then He must not know what
kind of man Craig was. There was no way in her mind that a
loving God could expect her to submit to *this* man.

Many women struggle with how to obey God's command
of submission because of situations like Sharon's. When we
are married to a man who does anything but reflect the image
of Christ, we will struggle to understand how to submit to
him. And when we can't come up with a viable answer, we
may decide that God must not expect submission to apply
in our situation. We convince ourselves that if God really
understood our situation or our husband, then He would
make allowances for this submission thing. We have justified not being submissive because of the man we are married
to. "Maybe I married the wrong man." Or, "I don't think God
had my husband in mind when He handed out His instructions." Here we are as strong-willed wives once again saying
we know better. Do we even know more than God? Ouch!

When the man we married is not behaving in a godly
manner—whether he is more passive or more strong
willed—we have to understand that God does know our
husband, our situation, our struggles, and our fears. And
that His commands still apply to both us and our husband.

Even if our husband hasn't obeyed the commands about how a husband should treat his wife, that doesn't give us the right to not do our part.

In his book *Marriage on the Rock,* Jimmy Evans states, "While it is true that many men in this generation have violated their roles of leadership in serous ways, that fact does not justify the ungodly and unbiblical response of many women."[1] We have to stop making excuses for *our* unbiblical behavior and spend that time instead figuring out how to change ourselves to benefit the marital relationship.

Maybe you didn't marry the most spiritual, loving, devoted man in the world. Maybe you really are married to a callous jerk. Maybe you can't imagine him loving you as Christ loves the church. Maybe you have convinced yourself that you have married the wrong man and you'll just have to live with it. If that's the case, you will likely feel trapped—not a good feeling for anyone to have. In these cases, the most powerful tool you have to break free of feeling trapped is your mindset. Motivational speaker Zig Ziglar has a great way of putting it:

It's possible you did marry the wrong person. However, if you treat the wrong person like the right person, you could well end up having married the right person after all. On the other hand, if you marry the right person and treat that person wrong, you certainly will have ended up marrying the wrong person. It's far more important to be the right kind of person than it is to marry the right person. In short, whether you married the right or wrong person is primarily up to you.[2]

I know that may sound Pollyanna-ish and is much easier said than done. It sounds great to say, "just start treating your frog of a husband like the prince you wish he were, and he will magically change into your Prince Charming." I agree that's not the fix-all. But it really is the place to start. Our mindset is more powerful than we realize, and it can set the stage for success or failure within a relationship.

Once we begin to adjust our mindset, we can better see both the positive and negative aspects of our relationship from a more realistic perspective. We can then evaluate how to apply the true meaning of submission. "Submitting" to Craig's sexual requests was not to the benefit of Sharon's marital union. It did nothing to bring a sense of oneness between them but actually separated them even further. Increasing the distance between couples is not at all what true submission is about. As your mindset adjusts, first look for a few areas of your marriage that are more positive and healthier and start working there. When we start looking, we can usually find some redeeming quality to focus on. As you identify these areas, even if they seem insignificant at the beginning, use these to work on demonstrating a submission toward your husband that shows your ultimate desire to have a healthy marriage.

In Sharon's case, she was able to identify Craig's work ethic and financial provision for the family as positive. Although it was difficult at first, because she was so focused on everything that was wrong with their relationship, eventually she was able to use this to encourage and compliment Craig. Over time she noticed more positive aspects, although we may never know if that was because she was looking deeper or because he was making changes. But I'd like to think it was both.

## EXCUSE 3: "WHEN HE STARTS DOING HIS PART, THEN I'LL START BEING SUBMISSIVE."

As Renee and Scott left church, he could tell she was fuming. He knew better than to ask what was bothering her, because the sermon had been on leadership and submission in the home, and that topic always got her riled up. Eight years of marriage told him her anger wouldn't just go away, but he didn't want to bring it up for a couple of reasons. First, he didn't want to listen to her soapbox speech about how pastors misinterpret submission. But even more, he was feeling personally convicted by some things the pastor had said. He realized through very specific illustrations the pastor used that he wasn't treating Renee the way he should. He often teased her about sensitive topics but covered himself by saying he was just joking. The pastor hit that one hard today and explained that no matter what his actions were toward his wife, his words could destroy her. He couldn't shake how bad this was making him feel, and he didn't want to talk about it yet. But the tension was building as they drove home, so he tentatively asked what she was thinking about.

Renee started her tirade about why preachers spend so much time talking about the wife needing to be submissive and so little time on how the husband is supposed to love his wife. "That part comes first in the Bible, doesn't it? And he just skims right over it and moves to the submission part! Doesn't he know that I *can't* be submissive to you if you aren't treating me the way you should? And you don't! Do you think Jesus would go out every weekend playing golf and leave his wife at home alone? Do you think Jesus would make his wife do all the work around the house when she's worked just as hard as he has all week? I don't think so! But I'm the one who's supposed to be submissive. Did he say anything about what you are supposed to do different today? No! It was all about me!"

When Renee came up for air, Scott tried to jump in and point out what the preacher had said to challenge husbands to better love their wives. But she would hear nothing of it. She was convinced the preacher and Scott were both telling her and only her to change. And she was set on convincing Scott that he was the one who needed to change first. "When you start treating me like I deserve to be treated, then I'll consider being more submissive, but not until you do. When you treat me like I'm a disposable commodity and not even important to you, then why should I submit? I'm the only one watching out for me."

I met Renee and Scott later that week in my counseling office. The tension was still high, and Renee had quite a chip on her shoulder. She had specifically requested a female therapist, hoping to have an ally and expecting any man to say what she perceived her preacher and husband to be saying. But although I sympathized with her hurts, I challenged her on one statement I heard her say: "I can't be submissive to you if you aren't treating me the way you should." This *can't* word was our jumping off point. We discussed personal responsibility: each person doing what God commanded him or her to do in the marriage, which is not dependent on whether the other is doing his or her part.

Scott admitted he wasn't showing Renee that he loved her through his actions and words. He said he wanted to change. Eventually Renee was also able to admit she wasn't doing her part. She truly believed that she didn't have to submit to Scott until he was acting like a godly husband, by her definition. As we gently challenged this mindset, Renee began to open up to what God was asking her to do without focusing on Scott's responsibility.

The excuse, "I don't have to until you do," is based in the belief that I shouldn't have to be the one to change first. How many of us strong-willed wives are sitting around thinking this? We blame someone else for the reason we aren't doing what we are supposed to be doing. "If he loved me like Christ loved the church, I'd have no problem submitting to him. But he doesn't, so I won't."

That just won't fly. Being submissive is not about finding one more new way to manipulate or try to change your husband. It's about showing your love for God through the way you obey His commands and relate to your husband. We are responsible for this regardless of the outcome. This is one of those times when we need to direct our strong-willed nature to work for us instead of against us. Instead of being stubborn and waiting for someone else to move first, why not use our desire to make changes and our ability to face challenges head-on to help us make the first move? We say we like to be trailblazers and to "win" at whatever we're doing. Well, "winning" usually means being first, so why not be first to change?

We need to show the positive aspects of our strong will and jump in to change ourselves whether or not our husband does his part. Then we can actively pray for God to begin moving our husband in the direction God chooses. It is not our job to be our husband's Holy Spirit. We need to get out of the way and let God do His job. We need to trust that God wants the best for our marriage just as much as we do. It will please God to see us making the necessary changes within ourselves for our marriage. And if we do our best to communicate openly with our husband about the changes we are making and about our need to work together on changes, we will likely begin to see changes in both of us. If that's not the case after open communication, prayer, and several months of work, then I believe that is the time to seek out professional counseling to help the two of you identify what's keeping you stuck.

## WHY I REALLY WON'T LET MY HUSBAND LEAD

As we have identified just a few of the excuses for not being more submissive, we have to realize that none of these holds any weight. We have to stop making excuses, because excuses won't fly on Judgment Day. Hasn't it been said that "the road to destruction is paved with good intentions"? We can have all the excuses and good intentions we want, but that won't justify us before God Almighty. There simply is just no excuse for rebellion against God's commands.

So, in order to move past our excuses, I think we need to spend time facing the fears that underlie our excuses. We make excuses because we are behaving in a way we know we shouldn't. (Otherwise there would be no need for the excuse, right?) So why are we behaving that way? Our actions are often tied to fears of what we believe will occur if we submit. Let's look at some of the things we may be afraid of.

### Fear of Losing Control

Donna is a perfectionist with a type-A personality. She has a particular way of doing things that helps keep her life in order and makes her feel more comfortable. Friends have teased her about being obsessive-compulsive because everything she does has to be organized and done "just so."

When she married Ron three years ago, she viewed this trait as a strength, but now she sees it causing stress in their relationship.

As they worked through the adjustments of their first year of marriage, she took on most of the household responsibilities, because she wanted them done her way. But it didn't take long for her to feel exhausted and resentful. The conflicts increased, but no solutions satisfied her. When Ron offered to take over something, she agreed only if he consented to doing it her way.

In one of their recent fights, Donna complained about Ron's spending. She accused him of having no idea how bad their finances were, and he responded, "That's because I'm not allowed to touch the checkbook!" She threw the checkbook at him and said, "Fine, there it is, you do it for a change!" As soon as the words were out of her mouth, she regretted having said them. She said she wasn't serious, but it was too late. Ron had grabbed the checkbook and headed to the desk for a calculator.

As she realized he was serious, she began instructing him how to go about managing the finances. She had an extensive and complicated system that included color coding each entry. She said if he couldn't do it her way, she would take it back.

I believe many of our excuses are related to our fear of losing control. We feel more comfortable when we are personally in control. We are self-reliant and don't believe we need anyone else. Being in control maintains our sense that everything will be done right. But when we aren't in control, that security gets shaky. We aren't convinced that things will work out the way we want or need them to. We truly believe "things are best when I'm in control."

And therefore, we don't allow our husband to be all he

can be. When we take over leadership, then we aren't letting our husband fulfill his God-given role. If our feet are in his shoes, then he can't step into them. No matter how bad we think our husband has become at leading, we shouldn't step outside God's design to fix it. It's not our job. We are responsible before God only for what He has asked us to do. On Judgment Day, I don't think God will say, "I understand why you didn't do what I told you to do. After all, you were so busy doing what I told your husband to do."

Control and intimacy are opposites. We cannot control someone and be intimate with him at the same time. If we want true intimacy with our spouse, we must stop trying to control him. As I have met with and counseled many couples struggling with these issues, I have seen many unbalanced relationships. Often when a strong-willed wife is involved, the marriage takes on more of a parent-child appearance than one of mutual respect and oneness. If you feel more like your husband's mother than his lover and teammate, then maybe that's because you are trying to keep control that isn't yours in the first place. We are not the one in control — God is. We have to learn to trust that He wants what is best for us and that obeying His commands is good for us as well.

It is also very important to fight past the myths we may hold about submission. These false beliefs likely fuel our fears. In the case of the fear of losing control, we need to remember that true biblical submission isn't an all-or-nothing process. We should not be in total control, but nor should we fear having no control. Being submissive involves working toward oneness and being a team where both of us are seeking the same outcome. It is not about letting go of all control. Learning to work *together* is the key to biblical submission in managing finances, running the home, making decisions, or any other aspect of marriage.

*Fear of Being Taken Advantage Of*
One of the biggest fears strong-willed wives talk about is the fear that if they let down their walls of protection and submit to their husbands, then they will in some way be taken advantage of.

"Do you have any idea what will happen if I go home and tell my husband that I'm going to work on being more submissive? First, he'll laugh his head off and say, 'You? Yeah, right!' And when he realizes I'm serious, he'll say something like, 'Okay, it's about time—now head to the bedroom and jump my bones.'"

"When I started learning about submission, I realized I needed to make some changes. I talked with my husband, and surprisingly he handled it maturely. At least at first. It didn't take long for the jabs to start being thrown my way. And these only came up when he wanted something I wasn't comfortable with and I said so. He seemed to believe that my submission meant that he would always get his way, whether it was going fishing every weekend with his buddies, buying an old gun at a pawn shop, or telling the kids to go to bed early so we could have some private time. It didn't matter what I felt or thought. He'd just say, 'You aren't being submissive.' I quickly got tired of that and wanted to stop trying."

"My experience with trying to be submissive made my marriage worse, not better. The more I talked to my husband about the changes I wanted to make and how I thought we needed to work together, the more he came back with, 'The Bible says I'm the head of this house, and that means I'm in charge and you need to listen to me!' I knew from what God was teaching me that his view of leadership and submission was not right, but how could I get him to see it differently?"

"I tried everything I knew. I had him read some of the same things I was reading, and I even bought a CD by a male pastor that he likes to listen to. But nothing changed. He actually became more of a jerk in how he treated me than he was when I did things my way.

"Letting go of control also brought other problems into the light and made me realize that my lack of submission wasn't the major problem. Lack of respect, selfishness, and a total ignorance of oneness in marriage surfaced, and I worried that our marriage would fail. My initial reaction was to go back to how things used to be, but God helped me see that wasn't the answer. Instead, I decided we needed professional help and I asked my husband to go to counseling with me. At first he refused, and I went alone a few times. But once he realized I was going with or without him, he decided to go with me. Things are still rough, but at least I have hope and we are working on some of the underlying issues."

A common fear for strong-willed wives is the fear that submission means they will be taken advantage of. We strong-willed wives tend to have a strength that helps keep us safe from being hurt—or at least that's what we believe. We fear being taken advantage of and therefore don't allow ourselves to be placed in a situation that is unknown or out of our control. What if we're more submissive, our husband takes advantage of that, and we get hurt? What if he asks us to do something we're not comfortable with? What if he uses submission against us and forces us to do what he says?

This fear is tied to several of the myths discussed in chapter 11. As long as we hold on to false beliefs, we will remain fearful. We need to remember here that submission is not about being forced to do anything. The myths that we will lose ourselves, have to do whatever our husband tells us to do, or have to endure abuse are the main myths fueling this fear. If you are married to a man who will want to use your submission against you, then you must consider that this mental manipulation is a form of psychological abuse that you shouldn't tolerate. It is likely that other more serious issues within your marriage will surface as you make changes. If so, you will need to seek counseling to help both of you adjust your ways of thinking and interacting with each other.

If you are married to a man who is not demonstrating these behaviors and yet your fears remain strong that he will, then the issue more likely lies within you. You may still be fighting the ghosts of your past and the expectations that you will be hurt again. We talked in chapter 4 about specific things to do to release the hold that your past may have on you. I encourage you to review that section and seek the help you need to alleviate this fear.

*Fear of Being Miserable*

Strong-willed wives equate "submission" with "torture." Whether we admit it or not, we believe that in order to be submissive we will have to become someone we are not. We fear losing our identity and significance. The concept is so contrary to who we are that we struggle to see anything positive in it. Why would God create us this way and then ask us to be someone we are not? But that's not what submission is about. God is not out to torture us or make us miserable. He wants the best for us. He sees the big picture and asks us to do the things that will benefit us and our relationships. The real question is not "Can we understand it?" but "Can we trust it?"

Consider times when as a parent you have to command your child to do something that you know is good for him but that he doesn't agree with. Like taking him to the doctor for shots or giving him medicine when he's sick. Does he believe you that this is really necessary for him to be healthy? Probably not. But you see the bigger picture, and you know what the results will be. God knows that some of the things He asks us to do aren't easy or pleasant at the moment. But the end result will be a healthier marriage. His commands are not only good, but good for us.

*It All Boils Down to Trust*

Kristen sat in my office apologizing for being hot and sweaty. She explained that she had just come from her workout with her personal trainer. She talked about how hard he had been working her. She had struggled with added weight since the birth of her second child and had decided this was the only way to get that weight off. "If I pay big bucks for this guy to run me ragged, maybe I'll stay motivated and get the results I want."

It was working. She was losing weight and getting back into shape. She occasionally complained about how hard the work was or about some crazy exercise he told her to do. If she argued with him about it, he just said, "If you want the results, then you have to do what I tell you to do." And she would contort her body in all sorts of painful ways just as he told her to do.

In therapy we had been working on some of Kristen's strong-willed issues and particularly about submission to her husband. She was struggling with this concept and couldn't believe a loving God would ask this of her. I saw a teaching opportunity. "Do you trust your personal trainer more than you do God?" I asked. I saw the light go on inside her head. Even though what her trainer was asking of her was hard, painful, and difficult to understand, she trusted his specific expertise and she did what he asked. Could she do that with God? Did she trust His expertise in relationships and marriage? Was she willing to do what He asked her to do even when it was difficult?

When we boil down our excuses and fears, we find the issue is trust. We don't trust anyone or anything as much as we trust ourselves. We believe in our way of thinking and doing things, and it's difficult to break out of that mindset. Regardless of how much we know our husbands love us, we still struggle to trust that they won't abuse their authority. But even more, we struggle to trust that God wants and knows what is best for us. We argue with both our God and our husband as to why this isn't necessary for us. We fight submission because of our fears. But can we learn to trust that God loves us and asks us to do something that in the long term will benefit our relationships as wife and mother?

Learning to trust is a hard process that requires a lot of

mind-over-matter thinking. If we have talked through our hurts from the past, tried to resolve these events that hinder us from trusting others, and worked to forgive those who have hurt us (see chapter 4), then rebuilding trust becomes an act of our will. We must be willing to take risks and give people a chance. We have to be willing to risk being vulnerable with those people whom we have allowed to be closest to us, because these are the people whom we have deemed to be at least somewhat trustworthy. And if we can see submission for what it really is and how we can say no and still have a submissive heart, we will be better able to take these risks without fear of being hurt, because that's not part of what biblical submission involves.

Most of our husbands are probably more trustworthy than we have allowed ourselves to believe, but as we let our wall down and let them in just a little closer and lean on them just a little more, then we will see that they really are there for us and want the best for us. We will experience love at a deeper level than we have likely allowed ourselves to experience in years.

## COMING UP NEXT

Even if we improve our ability to trust those closest to us, especially our husbands, we will likely still struggle with submission. Why? Because we simply don't *feel* like we want to submit. We live in a society that emphasizes how we feel, and most of us go about our daily lives making decisions based almost entirely on feelings. But if we wait until we *feel* like being submissive, it won't happen. So how do we override our feelings and do it anyway? That is the topic of the next chapter.

# CHAPTER 14

# I Don't Feel Like Submitting Today!

THE DECISION TO LOVE, honor, respect, and submit is just that—a decision. As much as many of us want to believe that our relationships are held together by *feeling* in love with each other, that's really not the case. I don't stay married to my husband because I wake up every morning feeling madly in love with him. I don't work to honor, respect, and even submit to him because I feel like it. I do all of these things because I choose to do them. I make a daily decision to act in ways that are either honoring and respectful or not. That is my choice. There are many days when I wake up not feeling "in love" or in the mood to submit at all. And I have the choice on those days to go with my feelings or rise above them.

How I feel is not the most important thing if I want a satisfying relationship. Our feelings are a huge part of who we are and why we choose to act the way we do. However, they should not be the most influential part. We should be able to make good choices regardless of our feelings.

## PUTTING FEELINGS IN THEIR PLACE

God understands that our feelings are real and often strong. He also knows, however, that feelings don't exist in a vacuum. They are closely related to what is happening around and in each of us. How we *think* about the world and the people in it is a huge contributor to our feelings. How we *act* and interact with our world is another. But if we don't understand that these other parts of ourselves—our thoughts and behaviors—influence our feelings, then we may give our feelings more power than they deserve.

Many people today make major decisions based almost entirely on how they feel. People choose to get married because they feel "in love," then later choose to divorce because they feel "out of love." People choose to quit their jobs because they feel bored and choose to have a baby because they feel lonely. Should such major, life-changing decisions be based on something that can change from minute to minute? How can we learn to accept our feelings without allowing them to control us and our decisions? How can we learn to act with obedience to God's Word even when we don't feel like it?

We strong-willed wives often let our powerful feelings dictate how we react to someone. To make healthier choices, we must learn to take control of our feelings. I doubt many of us will ever wake up and say to ourselves, "I feel like being submissive today." Does that mean we shouldn't do it? In our feeling-based society, we are told, "If it feels good, do it," and by implication, if it doesn't feel good then don't do it. I've heard people say:

- "If I do something that I really don't feel like doing then it's just not real."
- "It doesn't count if I'm being fake and don't really feel like doing it."
- "I'm not going to do something that I don't feel like doing, because I don't want to be a hypocrite."

Does anything there sound familiar? Have you allowed your feelings to have that much control over your behavior? To keep you from doing something that you should be doing simply because you don't feel like it at the moment? Regardless of the strength of your feelings, you still need to choose the right action.

In her book *How to Act Right When Your Spouse Acts Wrong*, Leslie Vernick writes, "Choosing to act right when we don't feel like it isn't hypocrisy; it's obedience. Making this choice, however, involves more than mere behavioral change. Obedience does not mean we learn to smile with love on the outside while screaming with hate on the inside. Our heart and our mind must be engaged as well, even if our emotions are reluctant."[1]

So if we want to act right even when we don't feel like it, we need to understand how to put our feelings into perspective. If God gave us these emotions that so easily control us, did He also give us some tips on how to control them? Of course He did. In Luke 12:34, Jesus gives us the key to understanding and controlling our feelings when He says, "Where your treasure is, there your heart will be also." Let's break this verse down.

What does it mean to "treasure" something? You show that you treasure something by the way you think and act toward it. The more of your time and energy you give it, the more evident it is that you consider it to be of high value. When you treasure something, you will not only treat it well, you will also think about it often and in a very positive way. You don't view something as a treasure and then think awful things about it. So "where your treasure is" refers to the thing of value that captures your time, energy, and positive thoughts.

"There your heart will be." This does not refer to a physical heart but rather to the inner core of a person, including her thoughts, will, and emotions. So if we put this all together, what do we get? "Where your treasure is, there your heart will be" loosely paraphrased by Debbie becomes something like: "Whatever you truly value, that will be the focus of your thoughts, actions, choices, and emotions."

The more positive time and energy we devote to something, the more positively we will feel about it. This shows how to take some control over our feelings. As we learn to control how we *act* and what we *think,* our *feelings* will begin to fall in line.

Easier said than done, I know. Let's look specifically at how this works with the falling-in-love feeling. When a couple says they feel in love, you can bet that feeling is based on very specific thoughts and actions. Their actions have likely included spending lots of time together, talking long into the evening, showing physical affection, and doing thoughtful little things for each other. Their thoughts have likely centered on how wonderful the other person is, what traits they like about each other, and how they can't wait to spend time together. When these positive thoughts and actions occur within the same time period, couples fall madly in love and often decide to get married. And as long as they keep "treasuring" that relationship—keeping their thoughts and actions focused on the positive—they can continue to feel in love. But if they stop treasuring their spouse and stop choosing to spend time and energy on their marriage, then the feelings change.

When we understand that feelings are the result of thoughts and behaviors, we place less emphasis on the feelings and more on what lies behind them. We realize that we can't control feelings directly. But we can control our thoughts and actions, and as a by-product, change our feelings.

Couples in successful marriages know the love that makes a marriage successful is not a feeling; it is a choice, a decision, a commitment. We can exert some control over that kind of love. Just as we decide to love our spouse, we also can decide to honor, respect, and submit to him. Waiting until we feel like it won't work. It is much less likely that our feelings will change how we act than it is that our choice to act will change how we feel.

I use a model to show how thoughts and behaviors can control feelings. Understanding this example can help us choose to act right even when we don't feel like it. You may have tried to control your actions and attitudes in the past, and your thoughts and feelings kept working to sway you negatively. If we first understand the source of our feelings, then we can exert some control over them. Then we gain power to make choices that are not based on emotions alone.

**THE TREASURING MODEL**

Luke 12:34, "Where your treasure is, there your heart will be also," is the basis of my model. Although the principle applies to just about any feeling that we have allowed to control us (sadness, depression, anger, happiness, and so on), let's look at the feeling or desire to be submissive.

For us strong-willed wives, as for most women, this feeling is not going to pop up very often. And no one can create a feeling out of nothing. Have you ever thought to tell someone who's feeling sad and depressed to "Just snap out of it and be happy"? That sounds ridiculous, doesn't it? Likewise, we can't just decide to feel submissive. So if we wait for the feeling to come, we will never move forward. But based on this model, we can move forward on how we choose to think and act, and then eventually the feelings will come around.

Inside, human beings are made up of our thoughts, feelings, and behaviors. We like these different parts of ourselves to fit together smoothly, to be consistent with each other. We also prefer to be relaxed and are most comfortable when there is no tension in our lives. The only way to avoid tension is to have consistency between our thoughts, feelings, and behaviors. When they all match up, we are in a comfortable and stable space. We like our lives and our relationships to be stable, although stable may not always mean healthy or satisfying.

For example, let's say you and your husband have worked out a relationship where each of your roles seems fairly stable. You as the strong-willed wife may take more control than is healthy and your husband may let you do that for whatever reason. You may be comfortable and stable, but that doesn't mean this is the type of relationship that God prefers for you. You may *feel* in control and secure, and your *thoughts* are likely to match those feelings. ("I'm doing what's best for my household." "I'm good at being in charge, so why not be in charge of everything?" "I don't need to be submissive as long as things are running smoothly this way.") In order to be consistent, your behaviors fall in line, making you driven, focused, controlling, and argumentative at times. When all three of these components agree, you are in a stable (but in this case, not healthy) state.

So in this example, even if your current state feels stable, how does change occur? By the conscious choice to change whatever parts of yourself that you can. We have already established that feelings are not something you can just snap out of. Therefore, the feeling point of our equation is not the place to start. *Feelings* will change as a result of your *thoughts* and *behaviors* changing. If you choose to wait to make changes until you feel like it, then no change will be made. When you are really ready for a change, you will need to change the two parts of yourself that you do have control over—your thoughts and behaviors—regardless of how you feel. Changing only one of these two will not give you the desired outcome. Understanding and focusing on this source of our feelings gives us power to exert some control over them.

If you choose to change only your *behaviors* and act submissive on the outside, but don't adjust your *thinking* about submission, then your efforts will likely be short-lived and ineffective. If you choose to adjust your *thinking* and yet don't show this in any of your *behaviors*, again no change will occur in your marriage. You must focus your effort on both your submissive behaviors *and* the thoughts and motives that drive those behaviors at the same time if you hope to make a true change in how you relate to your husband.

The process of changing only your *behavior* and allowing your *thoughts* to remain negative is what I call "faking it." Faking it to me is doing one thing on the outside but believing the opposite on the inside. This is a formula for disaster. If you determine to act submissive but allow negative thoughts to remain or have the wrong motivations or expectations, this will likely backfire on both you and your husband. When your actions don't give the result you thought they would, you end up feeling worse than before you tried to push yourself, and you'll want to retreat to what you did in the past.

Unfortunately, this is exactly where many of us get stuck.

Because it's easier to change our actions than to change the way we think, we often try this first in hopes that our thoughts will eventually catch up with our actions. Instead, we need to take time to evaluate our motives. Maybe we are acting differently, but only because we hope that we will get our desired outcome. We may hold on to underlying expectations that submission will make things work out our way. These expectations may not be conscious, and we may not become aware of them until after something hasn't worked out and we feel disappointed, frustrated, or even angry. We can convince ourselves that we are changing our behavior for the right reasons until God shows us what's hiding inside. That is exactly what happened to me while I was in the process of learning these concepts.

## SURELY HE'LL MAKE THE *RIGHT* DECISION

Our middle child, Tiara, had come home sick from school the day before. Jim had left the office where we work together to spend the rest of the day with her. She was running a fever and felt worse that evening. We discussed how to handle the next day at work and at home, expecting that Tiara would still be sick.

We each had a different focus. Jim's focus was on being responsible with our business. He had already missed one day of work and had things he needed to get done. He knew that I would be willing to stay home with her, but that would mean canceling several patients, and he hated to do that. My focus was on nurturing my daughter even if that meant canceling patients. She needed me, and I wanted to be there for her. My patients would understand.

As we discussed the possibilities, we reached a compromise

that we would each stay home half the day and switch at noon. That would give Jim time to catch up on his work and me time to take care of Tiara without having to cancel too many patients. I thought it was all worked out. But then morning came.

Tiara woke up feeling better. Not great, but better. Her fever was gone, and for Jim that changed everything we had decided the night before. He saw her as good to go. I did not. I also felt the need to remind him of the school policy that states a child is to be fever-free for twenty-four hours before returning to school. I wanted to follow this guideline and give Tiara some extra time to get back to normal. A new decision now had to be made as to whether Tiara was going back to school or staying home, and if she was staying home, who was staying with her.

Although I already knew what Jim wanted to do, I gave my opinion strongly. It wasn't until we had been arguing for several minutes that I remembered this book. I had been focusing my thoughts to trust Jim's ability to parent our children just as well as I would, even though he might do that differently. This was a perfect time for me to practice what I'd been learning, and I was blowing it. I stopped mid-sentence and said, "I need to let you make this decision. Just tell me what you want me to do, and I'll do it."

His response was not at all what I wanted. I wanted him to immediately make the decision (preferably the one I agreed with). But instead he got busy with other things. He avoided deciding by getting the other kids breakfast, helping Talon pick out his clothes, and loading the dishwasher. All the while, I impatiently awaited a verdict.

When I asked him what the plan was, he said he would stay home for the morning with Tiara, but left the rest unknown. I needed information, and he wasn't giving it. Internally I had questions: Was he planning for Tiara to go back to school at noon? Was he thinking of staying home all day? Was I supposed to come home at noon and relieve him? I needed to know, and I needed to know now! What was so hard about making a decision?

I took the other kids to school and headed to work, praying all the way. "Okay, God, I know I blew it this morning, but I really am going to let him make this decision. I'm trying so hard to learn to trust him and his decisions and to be submissive to him. I know I don't have to be in control of everything. He is capable of making good decisions. Oh, God, please help him make the *right* decision." And of course the right decision was for Tiara to stay home all day and for me to relieve him at noon.

I was sure that if I was obedient with this submission and respect stuff, if I focused on my behavior and on having the right attitude, and if I prayed about it, then it would all turn out the right way—my way. So I kept praying until my cell phone rang. It was Jim. He reviewed the options once again and told me how hard this decision was to make. My frustration was evident, and I made some jab: "Yes, it's a hard decision, but someone has to make it. And isn't that why you're the head of the household?" (Yeah, I know—not nice.) He continued to avoid and hesitate, and things escalated within me. "Just make a decision! I need to know what to do. I'll do whatever you say!" He said that he kept hearing me say those words but didn't feel I really meant them. He felt he was in a no-win situation, and by that point he probably was. He just wanted to make the right decision, which really meant that he was trying to figure out what I wanted him to decide so the conflict would be over. He kept throwing out possibilities, fishing for some signal from me as to which one I would accept so he could get out of this no-win, uncomfortable hot seat he found himself in. I wanted to rescue him from this mess and tell him the "right" thing to do. But I didn't, because I was sure God was telling him.

Finally, Jim said, "You just go to work, don't cancel any patients. Plan on working your normal schedule, and I will either stay home all day, or if she's better, I'll send her to school for the afternoon. There, a decision is made!"

I was screaming inside: *No, no, that's not the right choice!* But on the outside I got very quiet and said, "Fine," in a tone that I'm sure did not indicate my approval.

Jim apologized for struggling with the decision and said he would work on making these with less hesitation and turmoil. As we hung up, I was praying—complaining really—to God. "How could this have happened? I thought You were supposed to bless me for being obedient and submissive. You're supposed to tell Jim the *right* answer." What I was really saying was, "God, if I do this submission thing, I expect You to work it out just the way I would have." I still wanted things to turn out my way.

Doesn't that seem logical? If I do the right thing by being submissive, then God should honor that by making sure my husband does the right thing or makes the right choices. (That may sound ridiculous, but that's where I was at that moment.) God used this incident to reveal to me my underlying motivations. I saw being submissive as just one more avenue of getting my way. If I did what I was supposed to do, then surely God and Jim would reward me by doing things my way. What God taught me through this was that I am to submit—in this case, allow Jim space to be the leader in our marriage—regardless of the final decision. I must truly trust God and Jim. And even if the final decision is different from what I would have done, that doesn't mean it's wrong. I also needed to work on my submissive attitude. I had tried to change my behaviors and focus my thoughts on trusting Jim, but my thoughts had never really moved. Until I could learn to submit in both my actions and my thoughts, with no strings attached, I would not be doing what God was asking me to do.

My attempt at faking it because I thought I was supposed to do and say certain things ended with me more frustrated than before I ever tried. I found myself wanting to quit. *Why even try to do this if it's not going to work and is just making things harder?* But the only reason I determined that it didn't work was because I didn't get my way. I had to face that being submissive is not about getting my way. And I had to realize that as long as I was faking it by changing only my behaviors and not truly working on my thought process, then I would continue to be frustrated with the outcome.

## WHY DO IT?

I kept asking myself, *Why do this? Am I nuts? Things aren't going all that badly in my marriage, are they? Why not just let things stay the way they are? Besides, this is just too hard. It's not who I am. I'm not a submissive woman. Why can't I just accept that and move on?*

But God wouldn't stop tapping me on the shoulder and reminding me that He was the one telling me to work on this. He had a plan, and I needed to grow in some areas that were both good for me and difficult for me. I had the freedom to either obey or not. God wouldn't force me (or you) to do it. Making these changes is totally a voluntary decision and yet something that I knew I would be held accountable for on Judgment Day. There would be consequences for disobedience should I continue to choose that path.

I love my Savior, and I want to serve Him with everything in me. And through this process I was learning that serving and loving Him meant submitting to Him and obeying His commands, even if I didn't like or understand them.

I have learned so much about how God loves, teaches, and parents us through the process of parenting my own children. Whether or not you have children, you can see how this example relates to what God expects from us in the marriage relationship. How often do we as parents lay down a rule for our children that to them makes no sense? Do we take the rule away just because they don't see the necessity of it? Of course not. They are children and don't know what's best for them at this point. They don't realize how many of the things they learn now will affect them either positively or negatively in their future.

Although I often try to explain to my children why the rules are necessary, there are times when the answer is "Just because I said so." As a child I used to hate it when my parents said that. As a teenager I swore I would never say that to my own kids. Well, that changed pretty quickly after we had our first child. Sometimes "Just because I said so" really is the reason. And maybe God sometimes has rules that we are supposed to obey just because He says so. He is our authority, and we are supposed to trust through our thoughts and behaviors that He knows more than we do. He is a good parent and loves us. He wants good things for us. He doesn't set down laws and rules just to be mean but to grow us to a better place. It doesn't always mean that we will like doing it or that the outcome will make us feel happy. But it does mean that we will become more Christlike and more pleasing to God.

We may have been misled into thinking that marriage is about making us "happy." Gary Thomas, author of *Sacred Marriage*, challenges us on this by suggesting that marriage may not have been designed to make us happy but to make us holy.[2] What if God designed marriage to be a relationship that He could use to grow us to be more obedient and closer to Him? One where we would have to learn to rely totally on Him in order to make it work. Where we could put His commands into practice on a daily basis and show our love for Him by doing so. Where He could rub off our rough edges and make us more Christlike.

Even when you aren't sure you can do what God asks you to do, remember that God will not ask more of you than you can give. He is not asking you to change who you are—He is asking you to use your strong nature to honor Him and your husband. Don't limit yourself by your lack of faith. God is still working in each of us, and miracles happen. Through Christ all things are possible, even submissiveness in a strong-willed wife. If you believe it, you will be able to outperform your natural abilities, because it's not you doing it but Christ through you.

**"IF FAKING IT WON'T WORK, THEN WHAT DO I DO?"**

Faking it, or changing behaviors but not thoughts, doesn't work. Since that's the case, how can we hope to make effective changes? The answer goes back to Luke 12:34. We defined *treasuring* as involving both behaviors and thoughts.

This is much harder than faking it, because choosing to control and change what we think is harder than choosing to change how we behave. But, for effective change to occur, we must make both changes at the same time. That is the principle of treasuring.

We strong-willed wives could get hung up on either behaviors or thoughts, but we tend to do somewhat better with actions than thinking. We work to change how we act while holding on to fears and unrealistic expectations. But as long as we do that, we are refusing to let go of our security blanket and risk true intimacy with our husband. If we don't actively work to dispel our false thinking and fears, then we are waiting for something to prove them right. The first time we change a behavior and it doesn't work out the way we feel it should, then we fall back into our safety net and say, "See, I knew I couldn't trust him to. . ." You can fill in your own fear here, whether it's the fear of trusting him to do a certain thing right or to protect you from getting hurt or some other fear. When it doesn't work out, it only leads us to put our wall back up.

Once we take the risk to believe something different about ourselves, our husbands, our marriages, and our God, then we are on the path to healing. We will be able to change our behaviors with expectations that say, "I know this may be hard, but it will work the way God planned. I'm just going to keep at it until I get it right." What a great place to be!

**COMING UP NEXT**

Are you ready to make a real transformation? Understanding that changing your behaviors and the thoughts behind those behaviors together is the key to relinquishing control and applying biblical submission to your marital relationship. When you are ready to start applying the principle of treasuring to your relationship with your husband, then you are ready for the next chapter. In chapter 15 we will learn how to put all this theory into action. We will discuss specific steps to start implementing to bring your personality under God's control in order to honor Him and your husband.

# How to Relinquish Control

IN THE LAST FEW chapters you have identified excuses and fears, learned to put feelings in perspective, and examined the model of treasuring. Now it's time to put all of this together and move forward. This chapter will address some steps for letting go of unhealthy control within your marriage so that your husband can become the leader God intended him to be. These steps will include changes in both your behaviors and in your thoughts, because that's what real and lasting transformation requires.

## TALK OPENLY ABOUT WHAT YOU PLAN TO WORK ON

The number one thing, as you start to make changes, is to talk openly with your husband about the areas that you plan to work on. There are several reasons for this. First, if he is a believer, you can ask for his prayers as you learn to be obedient to God's Word regarding submission. He will not only know specifically how to pray for you, but he will also know in what areas to watch for you to make changes, and if he's the type of person who gives praise and encouragement, then he'll be ready and able to acknowledge your efforts. He may also make a comment the first time you fail, but do your best to keep focusing on your own responsibility before God and not on your husband's actions.

Another reason communication is so vital to the success of this process is so that he knows in what areas he must step up and do his part. This is not to manipulate him toward what you feel the leader should be doing but so that those areas where you are making changes do not slip through the cracks. When I started making these changes, I caused new problems because I failed to tell Jim about the areas from which I planned to step back.

I decided within myself to stop making lots of little decisions. Some of these were inconsequential and others should have been Jim's decisions. Things like whether or not to get an appetizer at a restaurant, or whether to accept another couple's dinner invitation, or whether the kids could have friends spend the night. I had realized that practically every time one of the kids asked a question, I was the one to answer. It didn't matter what the question was or who it was directed to, I still answered. The children even left the room their daddy was in to find me to ask a question that Jim could easily have answered. It got to be a joke that all we ever heard was "mommy, mommy, mommy." I was worn out by it, but I couldn't complain, because my actions had taught them to come to me.

This was the first thing that I decided needed to change if my husband was to be the true leader of our family. Jim is an excellent father, and I knew he was more than capable of deciding on our children's requests. I just never gave him the chance. So I decided to stop answering questions in situations where both Jim and I were present and either of us could answer. Unfortunately, I hadn't informed Jim that this was an area where I had decided to change. I just assumed that he knew I was working on giving him back his authority in the home and that he would automatically take over wherever I let go. But he didn't.

When the kids asked a question, I bit my tongue and waited for Jim to answer. But all I heard was silence. It was as if he didn't even hear them. I waited for what seemed like an eternity (probably about thirty seconds), and if the kids didn't repeat their question, I looked at Jim and said, "Aren't you going to answer?" Then either he answered or asked what the question was. This went on for several days until I couldn't stand it anymore. How was I supposed to let him make decisions if he didn't step up and make them? Finally, when he again ignored one of the kids' questions, I lost it. "Why aren't you answering their questions?" You know what his response was? "I thought you would." Ugh!

"Why am I even trying? What do you think I've been doing for the past week? I'm trying to give you more authority in our home. I haven't been answering the kids' questions so you will take over and do it, but every time I have to ask you to answer them. If you can't even do this littlest thing, how am I to know that you will do the big things?"

Jim looked at me like I was nuts. "What are you talking about? What do you mean you've been waiting for me to answer the kids? This is the first I've heard about that. You've just always answered them quicker than I ever could. How was I supposed to know that something had changed? Maybe it would be nice if you tell me when you're going to do something different and expect me to change too. That just might help!"

See what I mean. Not talking openly about the changes

you are planning to work on in your own behavior just might backfire. Your husband isn't a mind reader. He has learned to work with many of the same bad habits within your relationship that you have, and if you want to make changes that will affect him, you need to talk to him about them. Expecting him to just know is setting him up for failure. He won't know, and therefore he won't step in, and his inaction will only fuel your thinking that this will never work for the two of you. But if the two of you talk through the changes you need to make before you decide what they should be, you are much more likely to eventually see an improved marriage—although your goal is to be responsible to God, no matter what happens in your marriage.

As you talk to your husband about what types of changes he would like to see each of you make, don't assume that you have the right answers. He may have different areas that are important to him than you would expect. So if you change only where and when you think changes are needed, then aren't you still the one in control? Take time to ask your husband where he'd like to see changes, and then listen—really listen—to his responses.

Since you've been thinking about this already and working it through yourself, be careful how you spring this on your husband. When you share with him the areas that you want to work on, be sure to let him know that you will work to stop trying to control everything and to let him be in charge of things that should be under his authority. Don't assume you already know what those are. Talk to him about this. Tell him you know that you have been making decisions that he is capable of making. Let him know that relinquishing control is difficult for you. Not so much because you don't trust him (although that may be part of it and that's an attitude you can work on privately), but in large part because you will be breaking some long-standing habits. Also let him know that you need his help. You need him to actively be in the leader role and do things that he likely hasn't done or that you have fought him on in the past.

After he has told you about changes he would like to see within your marriage, encourage him by telling him that you trust that he can be the leader he was meant to be. You believe in both of your abilities to make these changes with God's help. Ask him if he thinks it would be helpful to talk about this periodically—this will give you an opportunity for discussion instead of feeling the need to remind him about the changes he's agreed to make.

## STOP DOING EVERYTHING

After you and your husband have talked about the areas where you both want to start making changes, then it's time to step back in those areas. You have been wearing yourself out for years trying to manage everyone and do everything. You have not been acting like a member of a two-person team but rather like a lone ranger. God has provided you with a capable teammate, so isn't it time that you started letting him play?

Perhaps right now you're yelling something like, "Debbie, what are you thinking? You don't know my husband! Even when I'm sick, I still have to tell him what to do and when to do it. I have to make sure everything's taken care of, or it just won't get done. And you think if he agrees to be the leader and I just tell him that means I need him to start helping me, he's going to do it? You must be nuts." Or, if your husband is also strong willed you may be arguing that he has never considered your wishes in past decisions unless you threw your weight around, so why would he start doing that now?

You may think that your husband is not going to accomplish anything, because you have never seen him do it before. Keep in mind that this isn't about getting him to do something your way. And maybe you've never seen him do a certain thing because there's never really been a need—you've always done it. Regardless of the reasons why you've been doing everything yourself, those around you have likely become dependent on your doing it all. They are accustomed to sitting back and waiting for you to do it—because you will. So you're right. You probably haven't seen your husband doing the things you need him to do, because by the time he would get around to it, you have already done it and moved on to something else. If your husband is the passive type, he will remain so as long as you continue to do it all. He won't have a chance to show you that he can and will participate with you as a teammate until you back off far enough to give him the space to do so. If your husband is also strong willed, he may pull away to prove that he is in control of himself when you act like you're trying to get him more involved.

How far you will have to back up will be different for every marriage. But I can assure you that it will be further than you are comfortable with. He most likely will not do things as fast as you might want him to or as fast as you would do it yourself. He may not make decisions as quickly as you would and he may not make the ones you're hoping for. But the key to this step is being patient and waiting. Not the type of waiting where you keep score by counting the seconds that go by while he doesn't make a move, but the kind that says, "I trust you to do what you told me you would do. I am willing to lovingly remind and encourage you if you want me to, but I'm not going to nag you about it. And I won't step in and do it unless you tell me that you need me to." That kind of patience is truly God-given.

## SET REALISTIC EXPECTATIONS FOR YOURSELF AND YOUR HUSBAND

Setting expectations is a huge part of changing the thoughts that go along with your behavior changes. The expectations you set for yourself—and the changes you make in the expectations you've set for your husband, whether previously they were conscious or not—will set the stage for how you view your future success and failure. If you expect perfection (we strong-willed wives tend to be perfectionists) from either yourself or your husband as you each try to change, then you set up yourself, your husband, and your marriage for disappointment. Not only will your husband not be perfect as he tries to learn about godly headship, but you also won't be perfect in your attempts to be respectful and submissive. And if he's not a believer, your expectation that he act like one can be damaging.

If you set realistic expectations, you are much more likely to see your successes as steps forward and your failures as learning experiences. Out of all the things I've set my mind to do throughout my life, I can tell you that this has been the most difficult. I'm sure a lot of the reason is that the others were usually things I really wanted to do, things my personal passions were driving me toward. They fit easily into my personality style and therefore were not as hard to get a grip on. But this is a whole new ball game. I never really wanted to allow my husband to lead. I just came to a place in my life where I knew I needed to do it. And it's so contrary to my basic personality that I have to make a conscious effort not to always run the show. If I expected perfection from myself in this, I would have given up trying a long time ago. Of course, I must also factor in my husband's desires and actions, which I need to learn to respond to appropriately. But I know that this is a process of learning and adjusting, and I'm doing my best to take it one step at a time. I encourage you to do the same.

Finally, be careful not to expect things always to work out the way you want. At first I expected that if I did my part, then God would make sure things worked out right (which, of course, meant my way). That expectation is both unrealistic and wrong. We are not to use submission as a tool to get our way. Submission motivated by manipulation is not biblical. We must be willing to evaluate our motives and be willing to let God reveal to us if there is something wrong there.

## TAKE OWNERSHIP OF YOUR BEHAVIORS

Taking ownership of your behaviors means that you will have to stop blaming others, stop denying the behaviors, and stop avoiding responsibility for your behaviors. All three of these are things that we strong-willed wives often do. We are quick to blame someone or something else if something goes wrong. We often deny we have done anything wrong and spend exorbitant amounts of energy explaining our behaviors. And many of us are experts at avoiding open responsibility for the consequences of our actions.

If we say "I'm sorry" at all, we are likely saying "I'm sorry too" only after someone else has said it first. That doesn't mean we are completely oblivious of the impact of our actions on those around us. It just means that we are slow to take ownership of the negative effects that are apparent to those around us.

I realize that not all of the problems within our marriages are our fault. I'm not asking you to take full responsibility for what's gone wrong. I'm simply asking you to learn to openly identify your part of the equation. Slowing down and taking time to look inside yourself and examine your thoughts and motives will help. This can be difficult for many of us simply because we don't do it often. But it's a good skill to learn. Consider getting alone and asking yourself things like:

- What just went wrong here?
- What did I do that played into it or maybe even caused it?
- What *really* was my goal here?
- How much of my goal was to be in control of the situation or just get my way?
- How did I manipulate the situation or my husband?
- What could I have done differently?

Once you have identified your part of the responsibility, stand up and admit it to your husband. Apologize and seek his forgiveness. Even though some parts of the problem are not your fault, your part is still your problem. And the only way to change that is for both you and your husband to accept ownership of your parts of the problem and to agree to work on changing them. You must begin with yourself.

## STOP CRITICIZING

Learning to control your tongue will make a huge difference. Not everything that comes into your mind has to come out of your mouth. And not everything you feel needs to be corrected really does. This doesn't mean you have to shut your mouth and never say a negative word again. You don't have to stuff all negative thoughts and feelings inside you. You definitely shouldn't store these negative comments as future ammunition. Instead, you learn to choose your battles.

We strong-willed wives tend to focus on our way of doing and saying things as the right way (and sometimes the only way). When people do it differently, we feel it necessary to correct them. Don't they want to know what we think is the right way to do it? No, they probably don't.

The key to this step is to learn to accept your husband's differences and to understand that different does not mean wrong. He is not you, and he is probably not even much like you. He thinks differently, processes information differently, prioritizes life differently, has different feelings, and acts differently. That doesn't make his way wrong. As soon as you realize that you can't and shouldn't want to change him into a male version of you, then you can start to look for and find his wonderful traits.

If you continue to criticize your husband's efforts or redo what he's done (which is just another way of saying, "it wasn't good enough"), you undermine your attempts to let him lead. Why would anyone want to do something for you if all they will hear is how they did it wrong? If you have been critical much of your marriage, your husband may have a hard time stepping in and really taking over even in the areas that he's best at. He's gun-shy. He expects you to jump in and criticize him as you have often done in the past. It will take some time for him to trust that it's safe to come out and try again. Your words of encouragement will help, but what will help even more is his seeing you hold your tongue from criticizing his efforts.

There will always be some negative issues that you have to address. But the majority of your verbal interactions should not focus on the negatives. Choosing your battles means seriously considering which things need to be said and which don't. And completely letting go of those that don't need to be addressed. Many things can go uncorrected without the world falling apart. Probably, the world would be a better place if we let a few more things slide.

And when you do have something that you feel needs to be addressed, be careful to say it in a healthy way, not just as a criticism. Learning to speak the truth in love can be a powerful skill.

## PRAISE OFTEN

Taking control of your mouth is a two-part process. Keeping your tongue from criticizing is one part. The other is getting your tongue to issue praise on a regular basis. We need to attend to the positives in our husband and say these out loud. When your husband does positive things, do you usually pass on by and wait to pounce on the next thing he does wrong? That needs to change! Instead, look for the good in this man that God has blessed you with, and be open with your praise.

If he remembers to tell you his brother is coming over, if he takes care of one of your chores for you, or if he makes a decision that you've been thinking about, how you respond will affect whether he ever wants to do it again. You can either point out what he missed, or you can focus on the fact that he stepped up and did it, whether or not he did it your way. Be truly thankful for his effort. He may look at you like you're crazy the first couple of times, but I promise, he will love it.

This consistent flow of praise between a husband and wife

helps us handle the times when more negative things need to be addressed. None of us is perfect, and therefore there will be times when constructive criticism is necessary. But "a spoonful of sugar helps the criticism go down." A stream of loving praise flowing between you makes it much easier to hear and respond to constructive criticism when it comes.

Catch your husband doing good. Make a conscious effort to look for things that he does or traits that you see in him that are praiseworthy, and shower him with these comments. Say things that let him know you trust and respect him and his ability to lead your household. These statements will make him start to feel like the man of the house again and like the man God created him to be.

## BECOME MORE OTHER-CENTERED

Strong-willed wives struggle with other-centeredness even if we don't admit it. When we don't keep our personality traits under the control of the Holy Spirit, we quickly become self-absorbed. We may even justify our words and actions in the name of self-expression. "I was just expressing myself, what's wrong with that?" Well, if it's done in a way that hurts others, then there is definitely something wrong with it.

Our conversations are often filled with "I" statements, such as: "I'm right." "I know how to handle this." "I can take care of myself." "I didn't do anything wrong."

Being more focused on self than on others is a barrier to intimacy. Remaining self-centered will keep you from submitting with both your behaviors and your thoughts. How do you respond when your husband tries to share with you about something you did that bothered or hurt him? Something that he feels you did wrong? Do you listen quietly and hear him all the way through with a heart that wants to understand so you can make changes? Or do you immediately become defensive and argumentative? Do you focus on explaining the reasons why you did what you did and how those reasons justify your actions? Do you interrupt him mid-sentence and change the focus to what he did wrong that caused you to respond the way you did? Do you want him to see it from your perspective instead?

With every bone in our bodies, strong-willed wives resist admitting that we have done something wrong. It's not that we believe we're perfect, even though we strive to be. It's more that we are so self-focused we can't see the other person's point of view. We can see quickly the rationales for why *we* do what we do, and we are therefore certain that we were not wrong in our actions or words. We are more interested in getting our spouse to see why what we did wasn't really wrong than we are in hearing what he's saying and understanding his feelings.

In order for submission to be godly, it must be an other-centered activity. In order for us to show true respect for our husband, we must learn to focus on what he says and needs more than on our own agendas. It can't be all about us. It's not about what we can get out of it, but should be about what we can give. And the most important things we can give to our husband are our honor and respect. This involves hearing and understanding what our husband needs from us and then giving that to him as only we can.

If you aren't sure what he needs from you, ask. Sit down and really listen to what he says he needs and wants from you. You may say that this is not the easiest thing in the world for you. You may ask him to give you just a couple of things to start with. If he shares everything he needs or feels he's been lacking from you, the list may be overwhelming. And if you aren't careful, you may begin to defend why you haven't done such-and-such or why you believe you really have done it and he just hasn't noticed. This is not the place for that conversation. Just ask and then shut your mouth and open your mind to listen. You may learn more than you ever imagined.

Becoming more other-centered than self-centered requires an absolute change of heart. Books, pastors, friends, and family can all tell you what to do and can influence your behavior, but only Christ can change your heart. In order for our behaviors to be pleasing to God, we need our hearts to change. We need to become new creatures in Christ. We need to develop such a close relationship with Christ that our hearts change and therefore the desires of our hearts also change. When this happens, we can embrace God's commands as good for us because we trust Him completely. We will then follow His decrees not as duties but as opportunities to show our love for Him. We can then focus more on showing His love to the people around us and serve them without thought to ourselves.

## STRIVE TOWARD UNITY

Finally, when it comes to decisions within your home, the ultimate goal needs to be unity. Biblical submission has as its ultimate goal a stronger and more intimate marital relationship. It's about blending into one flesh and setting aside our selfish desires. We are on the same team and working toward the same goal.

Many couples are more in competition with each other regarding who does what, or whose priorities trump whose, than they are working together as a team. If this describes you and your husband, then some major changes need to take place. What is your common goal, and how can you work toward it? Everything one of you does reflects on both of you. You don't stand alone.

Emily and Justin were a young married couple struggling financially. They both were very aware of their lack of financial resources, but Emily felt the pressure more than Justin. She managed the checkbook and paid most of the bills but always kept Justin in the loop as to where things were currently. At times he seemed very concerned, like when he helped her write out the checks that were due. He even talked about needing to be more careful about what they bought at the grocery store or how they couldn't afford to visit her family because of the price of gas.

But these concerns disappeared when he was in the mood to buy something. He was impulsive with a strong selfish streak. When he wanted something from ice cream to a new digital gaming system, he was determined to satisfy that desire regardless of the cost or consequences.

One morning he woke up in the mood for Krispy Kreme donuts, and he was determined to get them. He had several tactics under his belt and began using these one by one to get Emily to agree. He tried everything—asking gently, begging, pouting, rationalizing, arguing, appealing to her sweet tooth, criticizing, making false promises, and eventually yelling. Emily simply could not see the need for his latest craving and continued to respond with, "You know we can't afford that right now."

As Justin worked his way through his repertoire, the hateful comments began to fly back and forth.

"Why do you always have to act like my mother? I should

be able to go get donuts if I want to."

"Why do you always have to act like such a child? Why can't you be responsible and tell yourself no once in a while so I don't have to? You talked me into getting ice cream last night and promised me then that you wouldn't ask for anything else. Well that lasted a whole twelve hours."

"I thought I was supposed to be the head of this family and make the decisions. Why don't you ever submit to me?"

"Because if I did we would be in bankruptcy court right now."

The fighting continued until they both went to their own corners to lick their wounds. Justin did so with his hands full of Krispy Kremes.

Krispy Kremes may seem like a silly thing to have such a big argument over, but as you probably know, the fight wasn't really about donuts but about a pattern of selfishness that was plaguing their marriage. Emily had reached a point of no longer allowing Justin's spending habits to go unchecked. She was willing to stand firm for the marriage and for spending in a way that maintained their goal of "happily ever after." But that did not include Saturday morning donuts. She worried that Justin was seeing her as just unsubmissive and dictatorial, but that was not her heart at all. She wanted their marriage to be the best it could be, but she was not willing to sacrifice for immediate gratification.

So how would you categorize Emily's decision? How about Justin's? Do you believe that submission should have meant allowing Justin to have what he wanted? Would that have increased the intimacy within their marriage? Personally, I believe Emily was submitting to the original commitment they made to each other—the agreement to build a healthy, God-honoring marriage. The issue was not as much about leadership and submission as it was about selfishness and manipulation. And I suspect that these issues will continue in this relationship unless they seek counseling and get to the root of the selfishness that is blocking them from becoming one and working together toward the same goal.

When it comes to making decisions within a marriage, we need a plan of action that keeps us moving in the same direction. That plan can take several different forms as long as we come up with it together, both agree that it is a workable solution, and then follow through with it. Maybe the two of you have agreed that certain decisions fall more into your realm of expertise and therefore will be yours, and others fall more into your husband's realm of expertise and therefore will be his. You will still discuss these decisions. A good team always keeps communication open. But when a final decision needs to be made, you have agreed who will make it. That is one form of unity within the decision-making arena. You have both agreed to do it that way, and therefore you are unified.

In other situations, some decisions don't specifically fall within either of your areas of expertise, so you need to make them together. This can sometimes be a real challenge, especially for us strong-willed wives. We need to let minor issues go and use the following formula only for truly important issues of disagreement. The goal is still unity in the decision. I encourage you to discuss these issues openly and take time to listen to each other's point of view. Then agree to pray about the decision and come back together to discuss further. I'm speaking as an experienced marriage counselor here. If at that point the two of you are still not in agreement, continue the process for as long as seems logical.

During this stage, also take time to talk about and evaluate your personal motives for making the decision. Be willing to look at any selfishness that may underlie your decision. And be open to evaluating if the decision is directed toward the ultimate goal of improving the marital relationship or if it could be motivated by selfish desires that would work against increased marital intimacy.

If Emily and Justin had taken time to do this, I think it may have been possible to bring Justin's selfish motives into the light before the emotions got so heated. If Justin had been able to identify this side of himself and look at the consequences his decision could have on the relationship, it is much more likely that a joint decision could have been reached. If the time comes that the decision has to be made but agreement has not been reached, I suggest that the husband take the lead and make the final decision, doing so with the goal of oneness as his guide, not selfishness. If you have together established oneness as a goal, then you, speaking the truth in love, can remind him of that goal.

Now as hard as I know this will be for many of you, I encourage you to consider this. The actual decision is not the most important component here, but the attitude with which it is made. The husband needs to make his best decision, and we hope he will do so with an attitude that says, "I know this is hard for you, but I really think it's what's best for all of us." When this is the case, your job is to trust and follow his lead. However, if he's saying something like, "It's my choice, and I'm just going to do what I want to do," then he's violating his position of godly leadership, and you may have to choose to address the selfishness of his decision and how this affects your relationship. Choose your words lovingly and your battles carefully.

The covenant you made before God is about becoming one flesh, and the submission that you are commanded to do will honor that covenant, not destroy it. Giving in to a decision that you truly believe will lead to the breakdown of the marriage is not biblical submission. Giving in to a decision that shows poor stewardship of the resources God has provided you with is also not biblical submission. As a Christian, you hold a level of personal responsibility before God just as your husband does, and it is important that you take that responsibility seriously. But you must be cautious in making these decisions and be sure that your own selfish desires aren't fueling your dissent.

The attitude behind your behavior is crucial. If you allow your husband to make the decision and accept it with a loving and submissive attitude, then things are good. However, if you say you accept his decision but your attitude and actions are contrary, then you're not demonstrating godly submission. The attitude behind the decision will either bring unity and intimacy or divide you even further.

**COMING UP NEXT**

You now have focused on the skills to bring the negative aspects of your strong-willed personality under control. The challenge at this point is, will you do it? Will you take the risk to make a major life change? And if you do, what will happen? How will your marriage look as the way you and your husband relate to each other changes? And how will you respond when you or your husband fall short (and you will)? The next chapter will sketch the stages you will go through as you make changes in your own thoughts and behaviors and help you accept the times when these new skills seem awkward. You'll see how women who have already been using these skills are doing.

# CHAPTER 16

# What If My Husband Won't Lead?

FOR ME, ONE OF the most enjoyable parts of watching the Olympics is the in-depth interviews with athletes. I love hearing how they have always dreamed of competing at this level and how they've trained practically their whole lives for this moment. Most have sacrificed not only time and energy to follow their dream but also family, friends, homes, and careers. They are willing to do whatever it takes to reach their goals. I have never heard one person say, "Oh, I just started doing this a few weeks ago. I thought it looked like fun, so I gave it a try, and here I am at the Olympics." It just doesn't work that way.

If you want to acquire a new skill and do your best at it, you won't pick it up one day and have it mastered the next. I cannot truly know what kind of training Olympic athletes have to do or how hard it is. I have no idea how many hours they put in or how many bruises they encounter along the way. But I do know they don't do it overnight.

They make their sport look easy. They skate across the ice, ski down a mountain, or do amazing tricks on the half-pipe and make it all look effortless. But to get to the point of looking effortless, they've had to want it bad enough to work hard all along the way.

Do you want the best marriage you can have? Do you want it bad enough to put yourself into training? Are you really ready to give it all you've got for as long as it takes to master the skills? Then let the training begin!

Not all of your practice times will go well. Sometimes you'll say, "Yeah! I did it! That was great!" Other times you'll hobble away feeling hurt and discouraged, because it didn't work out the way you planned. Still, you'll need to be consistent in your efforts if you hope to win the prize of a godly marriage. Occasionally you may have to reach deep inside for the determination to try again.

Your training will pass through several stages. Even when you feel awkward in the process, through these stages you'll develop the skills we discussed in the previous chapter to the point that they become second nature. Let's look at the stages you will likely pass through as you start applying these new skills.

## STAGES OF NEW SKILL ACQUISITION

There are four stages of new skill acquisition people pass through when learning *any* new skill. For example, Taffeta, my oldest and very strong-willed daughter, went through each of these stages as she learned to ride her bike. Your time frame will, of course, be more extended.

*Stage 1: Initial Learning*
Taffeta decided she wanted to learn to ride a "big girl" bike. We went to at least five different stores (and most of them more than once) in search of the perfect bike with just the right color streamers hanging from the handlebars. Eventually,

we bought one. Her dad and I discussed with her the rules for riding a big-girl bike. She spent much more time than she wanted listening to the instructions about wearing a helmet, staying on the sidewalk, and crossing the street safely.

Then we talked about what she was supposed to do once she actually got on the bike, and how Daddy would be running beside her holding the back of the bike until she was ready to try it alone. Although mom and dad took this all very seriously, her six-year-old little mind didn't. She stood with her hands on her hips and her blue eyes rolling around, saying, "Okay, okay, I already know all that stuff. Let's just go do it!" We knew all she wanted to do was get outside and take off down the street. We also knew it wasn't as easy as she thought it would be.

This is where you are right now in learning a new skill. You have identified a need to learn something new. You purchased this book and are now reading it to learn more about yourself and the ways you can change to please God in your marriage. You are taking the time to get the full set of instructions, although you may feel like you just want to do it *now*. This is the stage where we gather and evaluate information, but it's also the stage we strong-willed wives are most likely to want to skip or do only halfway because we think we already know it all, or at least enough to get started. We want to get to work *doing* something, not just reading about it.

### Stage 2: Awkward Use

Taffeta decided she had enough information and was ready to try it out. She began to apply her new knowledge, but with a natural awkwardness that she didn't expect. Instead of just getting on and riding down the street, she wobbled and made wide shaky turns, just trying to keep from falling. She often looked back over her shoulder to be sure her father was still there hanging on to the bike. She spent more time looking back than forward.

"Daddy, don't let go! Don't let go!" she shouted. "I'm supposed to do *what*? This is too hard. I can't do it." Daddy encouraged her to keep trying and assured her that he wouldn't let go.

Her frustration at not being able to do it the first time (or the second, third, or fourth) increased. She dropped the bike in the driveway and stormed into the house, ready to give up. (Sound like any of us?) "I'll *never* get it! You can take that ugly old bike back to the store."

After she calmed down, we talked about how hard it can be to learn something new. We reminded her that frustration was normal, but if she really wanted to ride, it would take practice. We also said how good she would look riding that beautiful pink and purple big-girl bike. A few days later she was ready to try again.

This is the stage where most of us strong-willed wives seriously consider throwing in the towel. If it doesn't come easy, and it won't, why keep trying? We may find ourselves yelling to our heavenly Father, "Daddy, don't let go!" or "This is too hard! I don't think I can do it." But our Daddy assures us that He will help us through this and never let us go.

This stage requires lots of support and encouragement to keep from giving up. You will feel awkward, frustrated, or maybe just plain silly. It will help tremendously if you and your husband can take time to pray together and encourage each other on a regular basis. You are both trying to make unfamiliar adjustments. It is so easy to fall back into old patterns, so you'll need encouragement to get up and try again, especially when you think it will never work out. Enlist the prayers and support of Christian friends as well. Having a couple of other strong-willed wives around you as you are working to make these changes can be a great source of support and encouragement. If you are all willing to share both your successes and failures with each other, you will feel strengthened by knowing you aren't alone. At this stage, you will often have to remind yourself of what you are working toward. You may find yourself saying, "I'm supposed to do *what?*" The encouragement you give each other will be invaluable.

*Stage 3: Conscious Application*
In stage 3, you know the skills and they're beginning to come more naturally. "Daddy let go, and I kept going!" I heard from a very excited little redhead. Over the next several days, Daddy stood in the yard and watched. Taffeta was much less wobbly but still appeared tense. We could see her concentrating hard on what to do. She was beginning to see the benefit of this new form of transportation but was still most comfortable staying very close to home.

As you enter this stage, you will know what you are focusing on, but you may feel you have to constantly remind yourself to use these new skills. Eventually, you will see the benefits of these skills through the positive effects on your relationship. You will begin to see your husband from a new vantage point and be more able to focus on his positive traits. You may, however, still find yourself using the skills in the easier, safer, less critical areas of your marriage. You are still testing the waters to see if this submission thing will be okay. Can you trust your husband to do what he says he will do and not take advantage of your new mindset? It's hard not to look for his positive response even as you keep reminding yourself that your submission is not dependent on his response.

*Stage 4: Natural Use*

At this final stage, the new skills become almost second nature. Taffeta grabbed her bike, jumped on, and took off down the sidewalk without hesitation. She yelled, "I got it! I'm outta here!" She rode to a friend's house almost out of Daddy's view. She probably didn't even remember how she got there because she wasn't focused on the skills but on what she would do once she was there.

When you reach this stage, you will feel assured that you have developed a new habit. You will apply your new skills regularly and without much thought. They will feel natural, comfortable, and almost effortless. Likely your marriage will be healthier, and although you will still be just as strong willed as ever, you will feel you have learned to keep your personality traits in check and use them in a way that glorifies God and brings honor to your husband.

Stay patient with yourself and your husband as you progress through each of these stages. Remember that the prize at the end of the struggle is a marriage that honors God—a healthier, happier marriage.

**THREE REAL COUPLES**

I'd like to introduce you to three couples who have been trying to put the skills from chapter 15 into practice within their marriages. Three strong-willed wives all want to apply biblical submission within their marriage. They all struggle to overcome the negative views they have held about submission. But at the same time, they each want more than anything to show their love for their Savior through the way they interact with their husband. Each wife has been working on learning to acknowledge and accept her strong-willed traits, to see both the positive and negative aspects. Let's see how they are doing.

*"I just can't do this anymore!"*
Rachael and Jake have been married three years and have no children. They have been focused on getting out of college and starting their careers. Rachael is slightly older than Jake but feels old enough to be his mother much of the time. Although Jake is very intelligent, he doesn't have much common sense in her opinion. He can talk all day about current affairs in the Middle East, but he can't remember to stop to buy milk on the way home from work. She feels she has to call to remind him several times to do anything she asks him to do. But if one of his friends calls and asks him to help do something more than a week away, he never forgets.

He says he's worried about their finances, and anytime she wants to spend money, even on budgeted items, he gets upset. But he doesn't think twice about stopping at Starbucks every morning before work. She's tired of trying to hold it all together. She's tired of the nagging, the double standards, his selfishness and immaturity, and the fights these cause. But she believes if she doesn't nag or yell, he doesn't hear her. "Why do all the day-to-day events have to fall on my shoulders? Why can't he see that what he's doing is wrong? He makes me feel like his mother and then wants to have sex. I can't do this anymore!"

Jake doesn't mean to leave all the decisions on Rachael's shoulders, and most of the time doesn't even realize he has until she yells at him. He just wants to have some fun, which he feels he never got to do while he was growing up. His mother was emotionally unstable and did little around the house, so he and his two sisters had to be responsible at young ages. He never got to spend his own money on what he wanted to spend it on. Now he thinks it's his time to do what he wants with the money he earns. He likes Rachael taking over in most areas, because it gives him the freedom to be the kid he never got to be at home. But he doesn't like her telling him how to spend his money. He's tired of her yelling about every little thing. "I can't stand it anymore. Why can't she lighten up? Life should be fun, and this is definitely not fun!"

Rachael is working on her strong-willed nature and desire to be in control. She sees she has in part created her own monster. She feels secure when she's the one managing the money and making the decisions and never considered it would ever be any other way. Until recently, anytime Jake offered to help, she told him she didn't need any help. So he went about his business doing something he enjoyed. Then later he'd hear about how he wasn't helping out or how he was blowing their budget.

Early in their dating, she realized that she could get Jake to do or not do just about anything she wanted if she nagged long enough or yelled loud enough. She got good at telling him what to do and stopped asking him what he wanted to do. Now that she's admitting this out loud, she hears how bad it sounds. The more she sees how she has been treating him, the more she wants to change. Yet she's terrified that change will mean disaster for them, especially financially.

When Rachael sat down and talked to Jake about what she was feeling and how she felt something needed to change, he was pleasantly surprised. He said he was tired of fighting and feeling like a child in his marriage. She had to bite her tongue not to say, "But you've been acting like a child." (She was learning that everything she thinks doesn't have to be said.) Jake felt he could be more responsible but stopped trying, because nothing ever seemed good enough for her. Rachael admitted that she was quick to point out everything Jake did wrong and almost nothing he did right. She committed to changing that.

They talked about areas they needed to adjust and decided the first big step would be to discuss their finances and to work out a budget *together.* They agreed that Rachael was better at managing the money, but they saw no reason why they couldn't make the budget together instead of Rachael just telling Jake what he could spend. They set a date to work out the budget.

When that date came, Rachael had already organized all the bills, written down what was due when and how much it was, and typed up a "working budget" for Jake to look over and "approve." Jake stormed out of the room yelling, "This is never going to work! You can't let me do anything, can you?"

Rachael sat there stunned. She thought he'd be thrilled that she had already done most of the work so they could get through this quickly and move on to the next thing. She thought she was doing so much better with her control and was letting him help. He could approve the budget. What more did he want? She followed him out of the room yelling just that.

The fight escalated and continued for almost an hour. Both said hurtful things about control and laziness, nagging and immaturity, leadership and submission, and before it was over, bankruptcy and divorce. It got nasty, and eventually they wore themselves out and called a truce for the night. Each went to a corner to lick their wounds, cry, and pray.

The next morning they awoke with better attitudes and forgiving hearts, but they were both still wounded and the tension was thick. Neither had slept much. Rachael had realized in the middle of the night that even in saying she would release some control to Jake, she had set things up so they would still go her way in the end. She was offering him nothing more than being a figurehead of the home, not the leader. She admitted aloud that she had totally blown it last night but was willing to try again. She was frustrated but wasn't ready to throw in the towel on submission. She was willing to try again if Jake was. And he was.

*"He doesn't need me anyway."*
We've noted that submission involves knowing your husband and his needs and then doing everything in your power to meet those needs as only you can. That's one of the parts of submission that I continue to mess up over and over.

As I was writing this book, I reached a point where I was close to my deadline and still had a long way to go. I was so far behind for several reasons, but mainly because my focus had been on something else that I wanted to do even more than write this book. We were adopting a baby! That was exciting, and this book was hard work. So when I had the choice where to spend my energy, I chose preparing for baby Trayton.

Trayton came home about two weeks before my book was due to my editor. It still wasn't done. Jim and I both knew these last two weeks would be hard on everyone, and we talked about the best way to manage. He agreed to take additional time off work to be home with the baby while I hid upstairs writing every moment that I could spare. I took breaks every couple of hours to spend time with Trayton and help with his continued adjustment to his new environment. We thought we had it all under control.

By the middle of the second week, with the pressure of the deadline breathing down my neck, I felt more stressed than ever. I took breaks to spend time with Trayton and our other three children just to get away from my laptop for a while. I interacted briefly with Jim, but mainly I gave what little energy I had to the children, thinking, *They really need me. Jim will be fine. He understands what I'm doing. The kids don't.*

I was wrong. Jim was wilting, both from lack of sleep and lack of attention from me. He was focused on giving everything possible to me and making my life easier so I could finish this book. And I was just as focused on me, which meant that he wasn't getting anything back and was running on fumes.

At one point I came up for air long enough to notice a certain look on his face. When I asked what was wrong, he said, "I'm just missing you."

I heard what he said, but I really wasn't listening. I responded by getting defensive and rationalizing why I wasn't there for him right then. "You know I'm crazy busy and stressed about this book. It's due Friday, and then things can get back to normal. Just be patient with me one more week. Besides, you agreed with me about accepting this deadline, knowing it would be really hard to make happen. You knew what we were getting into."

It was more important to me to justify why I was neglecting my husband than it was to hear his feelings and meet his needs. He watched me take time away from writing for everyone but him, and he was missing his wife. He wasn't even asking me for anything. He was just telling me how he felt. But instead of listening, I chose to defend myself and caused him to wilt just a little more.

It took me awhile, but eventually I realized where I had messed up and did my best to make it right. I stopped what I was doing and took a break just for him. I even apologized for neglecting him (see, I'm learning too). I said I knew I wasn't making him my priority, but that was going to change. It was amazing to me how much better Jim looked the rest of the day. Giving him some of my undivided attention and making him know how important he was to me did both of us a world of good.

*"It's starting to work!"*
Bev was thrilled when she and Charles decided that she would stay home with their kids until they went to school. She loves being a full-time mom to her three children, the oldest of whom just started school this year. She's thankful that Charles's job pays well enough to allow this, and she doesn't mind making a few financial concessions to make it work. She's so good with money and thrifty in her shopping that she seldom feels she or the kids have to go without something.

Her only complaint was that Charles wasn't as involved in the home as she thought he should be. She thought she had always been the stronger of the two of them and better at making decisions. But she came to feel she was doing it all. Charles fixed his own breakfast and left for work. He didn't return home until dinner was practically on the table. He spent the rest of the evening watching TV with a glance now and then toward the kids if they bugged him enough to capture his attention. Meanwhile, Bev picked up after the kids, finished laundry, got kids bathed, and put them to bed.

When she complained, Charles helped with one bath.

Soon he went to Bev and said, "Emily's crying. She only wants you to wash her hair. I don't know how to do it like you do." He went back to the TV.

One night recently, Bev had plans to go out with a few of the other moms from church. She was thrilled to get out but then realized how exhausted she always was before an evening with friends. In the past when Bev had plans to go out, Charles appeared helpless to care for the kids. "What am I supposed to feed them? What time do they go to bed? How am I supposed to give them all a bath?" The questions were endless, and previously she ended up doing everything she could before she left so he wouldn't have to worry about it. She prepared a healthy meal and left it in the fridge. She bathed the kids early and left a note of instructions a page long. It took so much energy that she rarely went out.

But Bev was learning about her need to be in control and her belief that no one could take care of her kids or her home as well as she could. She knew she was partially responsible for Charles's helplessness. In the past, anytime he did something on his own to surprise her, like clean up the kitchen, she complained that he didn't put the dishes where they belonged and now she couldn't find a thing. Before long he didn't do anything around the house, because he said she seemed to like it better that way. He felt like nothing he ever did was good enough for her. And maybe it had been true in the past, but now she was out to change that.

Bev was learning to trust Charles to be a capable and loving father, so she headed out for the night without preparing the way for him. She did say she knew he didn't need her to tell him how to manage his evening with the kids and so she wasn't going to. She trusted him and knew that he and the children would have a great evening together just as she was planning to have a great time with her friends. He seemed shocked as she left the house with no instructions and no meal prepared.

While she was out, she told some of the other moms what she had done and how hard this was for her. She was dying to call the house and make sure everything was okay or to tell Charles what he could fix for dinner or when to get them to bed. It was driving her crazy not to know what was going on. Luckily, this group of women told her not to worry about it. Charles was a good dad and could handle this just fine. She wasn't convinced but was determined not to call.

She had a great time, and when she arrived home, she said a quick prayer and asked God to help her stay positive and see the good in how Charles handled the night. She didn't want to be critical and knew that she would need God's help.

When she walked into the house, the kitchen was a mess, and she could see the remnants of corn dogs and chips on plates. Not at all what she considered a healthy meal. She started to make a mental list of things that were wrong. Then she got that tap on the shoulder that only the Holy Spirit can give and remembered different doesn't mean wrong. She needed to be thankful that Charles fed the kids on his own. It wouldn't hurt them to eat corn dogs every now and then. And if she thought it would, why did she buy them and put them in the freezer?

In the living room she found Charles snoring in the recliner with their youngest on his lap sound asleep. The other two kids were in bed together (even though they had their own rooms) with wet hair and sleeping in summer pajamas. The mental list started again: *It's 23 degrees outside, and he has them in summer pajamas and their hair still wet.*

*Doesn't he care that they might catch a cold? Why aren't they in their own beds? Why is he asleep, and the dishes aren't even done?*

Again there was that tap on the shoulder. She reminded herself to look for and share the positives. She covered the kids with an extra blanket and headed back to the living room. When Charles woke up, she met him with a smile and a kiss and thanked him for taking care of things while she was out. She specifically thanked him for remembering that tonight was bath night and giving the kids their baths. Her couple of statements of appreciation puffed Charles right up. He smiled and said, "It wasn't so bad. We actually had a good time tonight. We had corn dogs and chips and made it a picnic in the living room. Josh said he was glad there were no ants at our picnic." He was beaming as he shared about his "daddy time" with the kids, and Bev was glad she hadn't missed hearing about it by complaining. She could see that changes were happening, and they would be good.

**COMING UP NEXT**

Change is hard. My hope for you is that as you experience the inevitable failures, you will be willing to forgive yourself and your husband and try again. Few mistakes are unfixable. Usually all that is required is a sincere apology that takes responsibility for what you did wrong and states what you will do differently next time. It really does go a long way to also say you're sorry and are committed to keep working. Talking through setbacks without attacking each other will be extremely helpful as well.

There may be days when you don't feel like trying. Remember that your feelings should not govern your decisions. And when you don't feel strong enough to fight against your strong personality, remember that God will give you the strength to make these changes if you ask Him to do so. He may not give you a huge dose of willpower and motivation all at once. If you are waiting for that lightning bolt of "want to" to strike you, you may be waiting a very long time. But God does promise to provide for your needs. He seems to give me just the amount I need to take the next baby step or leap of faith. I often want Him to give me all I'll need to see this through to the end. But He tends to give me just enough for the very moment I need it. Nothing more. Nothing less.

As we wrap up, let's celebrate each other's strengths. We are all uniquely created with different talents. We need to be careful not to be governed by society's stereotypes for ourselves or our husband as far as who does what within the relationship, but instead to get to know each other's strengths and use them to benefit the team. Submission is not as much about division of labor as it is about the attitude of the relationship.

In the next chapter, I'd like you to imagine how you and your husband can complement each other. His strengths complement your weaknesses, and his weaknesses may be there to grow you stronger and closer to God. God has provided the perfect spouse for you to grow more like Him.

# CHAPTER 17

# Celebrating Each Other's Strengths

MAGGIE AND MAX ARE anything but a traditional couple. They have role reversal issues in every area. Physically, Maggie is tall, trim, and muscular. Max is five inches shorter and much more rotund. Maggie is always professionally dressed and well kept, but Max prefers sweats and an old T-shirt. Even at church, the most dressed-up Max ever gets is jeans and a nice pullover shirt. It's just his style.

Maggie has served two terms in the US Navy and is now a captain on the local police department. She enjoys carrying a gun and is an expert marksman. She is mechanically inclined and likes to drive fast. When she's not on patrol, she can usually be found in her garage tinkering with the stock car she has recently acquired and has started racing on weekends. But her favorite vehicle is her Harley-Davidson. She has enjoyed riding motorcycles since she was a kid and would never want to give it up.

Max, on the other hand, has no interest in any of those things. He's docile and enjoys reading, Bible study, gardening, and horticulture. In the spring their yard is the best looking in their neighborhood because of the care Max gives it. He loves shaping hedges and choosing just the right flower combination for each bed. His garden is weed free, and he takes pride in his veggies. He is an amazing cook and enjoys coming up with his own recipes. His salsa of homegrown ingredients has won first prize in the county fair two years in a row. Max has served as a deacon and Bible study teacher at their church for several years. The hours he spends in the Word have helped him bring Scripture to life for those he teaches. He also teaches his children Scripture and encourages everyone in the house to memorize at least one verse each week.

Because of their nontraditional interests and roles around the house, they have often been razed by friends and family, but they just shrug it off and say, "We like it this way." And they really do. They are both very comfortable in their own skin. They know who they are and complement each other perfectly, although not traditionally. This comfort is also noticeable in the way they talk about each other. Both Max and Maggie are quick to sing the praises of the other to anyone who will listen. They share how they appreciate the roles the other serves even though they know they are different from the norm. Through many long conversations, they have learned what works best for them and they stick with it.

A couple of years ago Max lost his job to downsizing. He was not as devastated as some of his coworkers were, because to him it was just a job. One of many he had held throughout his life. He didn't see it as a career—he just held down a healthy job to help pay the bills. But he and Maggie knew that if he had his way, he would much prefer to stay home with the kids. Anytime the kids were sick and couldn't go to day care, Max volunteered to take a day off work. He loved his kids, and any time he got to spend with them was wonderful, even if they were sick. This worked well for Maggie, because time off work from her job was not easy to take. Lots of people relied on her, and she loved what she did.

When the layoff occurred, Max and Maggie weighed their options. They both liked the idea of the kids not being in day care and Max staying home with them at least temporarily. They knew this decision would only increase the teasing comments they were already receiving, but Max said he would be proud to be known as "Mr. Mom," because he valued raising his kids more than anything. Because Max had always been in charge of the finances, he told Maggie how this change would affect their budget. As they discussed their budget, they realized that the money they would save by not paying daycare would balance more than half of the income they would lose. Max felt they could manage the rest by cutting back on nonessentials, and Maggie agreed. Once that was solved, they were both excited about the upcoming changes.

## DON'T JUDGE TOO QUICKLY

When you look at this couple from the outside, some people might think they need to read Christian books more than any of us. They seem to have their relationship topsy-turvy. How could God possibly be honored in a relationship that is so seemingly backward? Maybe the problem is our vantage point. We are outside looking in. From that perspective, there's no way we can see the inner workings of how Max and Maggie relate to each other. Yet we may be quick to pass judgment and assume that Maggie is in charge while Max is a submissive husband. Based on stereotypes of the roles men and women should have in a good Christian marriage, some people decide this couple doesn't understand what the Bible says about headship and submission.

But if you think that, I'm here to tell you that you are wrong. I agree that few pastors would choose Max and Maggie's relationship as a sermon illustration when they are preaching on Ephesians 5. Within our churches, just as in society at large, we still hold to some strong beliefs that there's a right way to have a godly, submissive marriage. If we allow church culture—or anyone—to dictate to us the right way to have a God-honoring marriage, we will miss what God has in store for us. What if His plan for your marriage doesn't look like what your pastor or the media or any other influence says it should look like? Who will you believe and follow? Will you be strong enough to stand up against society or other influences and do what God calls you to do?

Consider Glenn Zaephel's comments on this: "As with the whole of Christianity, the concept of submission must contain balance. We are to be submissive to the right things and nonsubmissive to the wrong things. And the right and wrong things are not so easily detected—especially at face value."[1] We must be careful to be slow to judge others' behaviors as submissive or not. We aren't in their shoes, don't live in their home, and likely don't know the whole story. Outward appearances can be deceitful. This is especially true if societal stereotypes influence us.

Max and Maggie believe they have reached a place of honoring God and each other. But they didn't reach this place overnight. Because they are both secure in who they are as individuals, they had to work to understand each other's God-given strengths, and this was not without bruises along the way. They have reached the place where they are willing to acknowledge that they don't fit any stereotype, and yet are not willing to be forced into a pigeonhole just because anyone says they should. They allow God to use what He created in each of them to make their marriage the best it can be. They agree that Maggie's strong-willed personality was difficult for them early on and sparked many fights. But as Maggie came to realize that this strong-willed side of her was damaging her marriage, she determined to make changes. Now Maggie and Max agree that even though Maggie is just as strong willed as ever, Max is the leader in their home. He guides their family spiritually, financially, and in many other ways, yet he feels no need to prove that to anyone.

Maggie feels secure in his leadership, because she knows he respects and values her. He sees her strengths and is comfortable delegating to her and allowing her to be all she can be. That makes it easier for her to submit to his leadership and to respect him for how he manages their family and their home. They are content before the Lord, knowing that submission is not about what others tell them to do but about what God tells them to do. They have talked and prayed often to find a place they both are comfortable with.

## STRIKING A BALANCE

On the playground in grade school, my friends and I used to stand on opposite ends of a teeter-totter and try to make it balance. Where I had to stand on my end of the teeter-totter was different depending on which of my friends was on the other end. Because each combination of the two people had different weight and mass, each balancing act looked slightly different.

Marriage is a lot like that. Because each person has a unique personality, and unique talents, strengths, and weaknesses, each marriage combination will also be unique. As we work together to reach a place of balance with leadership and submission, personality and talents, we need to remember that where we ultimately stand on our teeter-totter to bring balance will look different from any other couple.

Striking a balance within your marriage requires knowing each other so well that we understand our husband's wants and needs and are aware of his strengths and weaknesses. We need to take the time to talk and listen to learn how our personality affects the relationship. Once the two of us agree how God has gifted each of us, we then use these gifts to benefit the relationship, even if our marriage looks different from other people's.

We must decide to stop comparing ourselves and our marriages to anyone else's. Haven't these comparisons caused enough trouble? We strong-willed wives have struggled to feel we fit in or are doing it right compared to those "good Christian marriages" out there. We felt there must be something wrong with us. But I hope by now you have realized that's not it at all. The positive aspects of our strong personalities can be strengths we bring into a marriage. As long as we are willing to commit our personality to Christ's leadership, and let Him help us keep the positive traits from turning negative, we can use it to bring honor to Him and our husband. And just because that doesn't look like every other marriage out there doesn't mean that yours is not godly.

We strong-willed wives can have difficulty accepting that there is no right or wrong way to do this. In part this is because we have probably long ago already determined what the right way is, not only for our marriage but for everyone else's. We need to drop this presumption and replace it with God's plan for our marriage. The specific behaviors that are submissive in one marital relationship may not be so in another. If we focus on figuring out the right specific behaviors that will make us submissive, then we'll get stuck and won't reach the goal.

Let's say there are six specific skills needed to make a home and marriage run efficiently. Furthermore, let's say our culture says husbands and wives must both be able to do at least 5 out of 6. Our churches have set a standard that a husband should do skills 1, 2, and 3 and a wife should do 4, 5, and 6. When this equation is followed, the marriage is supposedly godly.

So what happens if a wife is much better at 1, 2, and 3 and the husband excels at 4, 5, and 6? Should they settle for lower advantages within their marriage just to keep with the set standards? I don't think so! I believe that when we try to deny or hide our God-given strengths in an attempt to do what someone else says, then we are rebelling against what God intended for our marriage. Additionally, refusing to bring our strong-willed personality under the management of the Holy Spirit to develop a submissive heart is also rebellion.

Honoring God and our husband is not about the right behaviors; it's about our heart attitude. It's about accepting that each of us has weaknesses, and ours may be the ease with which our personality can hurt others. And it's about opening up to our husband and working together to find out what we believe God wants for our relationship. Finally, it's about allowing God to look deep inside us and show us where we need to change and then doing so.

## TRUSTING GOD

We need to be willing to hand over to God not only the management of our personality traits but also all of our fears, misconceptions, stereotypes, and expectations. Then we must be willing to hand over our husband to Him as well.

God provided you with the perfect mate for you. He provided within your husband just the right combinations of pros and cons to make you grow into the person He wants you to be. I like the way Gary Thomas puts it: "Marriage is more than a sacred covenant with another person. It is a spiritual discipline designed to help you know God better, trust him more fully, and love him more deeply."[2] When you decide to trust this, you will stop trying to change your husband to be what you think you really need. He came with strengths to complement your weaknesses and with weaknesses that will rub off your rough edges and sharpen you to become more Christlike.

I hope that by now *submission* is no longer a dirty word in your vocabulary. I pray that you will continue to work to bring your fiery passion under control so that it can warm the hearts of those around you. I encourage you to find other strong-willed wives who are striving to learn and apply the same things you are. Loving, supportive friends who can lift you up when you fall and will help you reach your goals. I know these changes are difficult and will take time, but I promise that they are worth the effort. Anytime we are willing to surrender another aspect of our flesh to the Holy Spirit, He is faithful to strengthen us along the way. The blessing we receive is a marriage that brings honor to God and our husband.

# Notes

## Chapter 4: Where Personality Comes From

1. Florence Littauer, *Personality Plus: How to Understand Others by Understanding Yourself* (Old Tappan, NJ: Revell, 1983).
2. William Miller and Kathleen Jackson, *Practical Psychology for Pastors* (Englewood, NJ: Prentice-Hall, 1985), 42.

## Chapter 5: Culture vs. God's Pattern for Marriage

1. Dennis Rainey, *Lonely Husbands, Lonely Wives: Rekindling Intimacy in Every Marriage* (Dallas, TX: Word, 1989).
2. Rainey, 39.
3. James Dobson, *Bringing up Boys* (Wheaton, IL: Tyndale, 2001), 161-162.
4. As quoted in Dobson, *Bringing up Boys*, 14.
5. David Gushee, "A Crumbling Institution: How Social Revolutions Cracked the Pillars of Marriage," *Christianity Today*, September 1, 2004.
6. Dobson, *Bringing up Boys*; Darien Cooper, *You Can Be the Wife of a Happy Husband* (Wheaton, IL: Victor, 1977); James Dobson, "Special Section on Marriage and the Family," *Christian Counseling Today*, vol. 11, no. 3 (2003), 36-38; Carol Kent, *Secret Passions of the Christian Woman* (Colorado Springs, CO: NavPress, 1990).

## Chapter 7: The Strong-Willed Woman Chooses a Man

1. Nancy Groom, *Married Without Masks: A New Look at Submission and Authority* (Grand Rapids, MI: Baker, 1996), 57.

## Chapter 10: As to the Lord: A Wife's Responsibilities

1. *New Webster's Dictionary of the English Language; College Edition* (New York: Consolidated Book Publishers, 1975), 1278.
2. Darien Cooper, *You Can Be the Wife of a Happy Husband* (Wheaton, IL: Victor, 1977), 76.

## Chapter 13: Why Won't I Let Him Lead?

1. Jimmy Evans, *Marriage on the Rock: God's Design for Your Dream Marriage* (Tulsa, OK: Vincom, Inc., 1992), 76.
2. Zig Ziglar, *Courtship After Marriage* (New York: Ballantine Books, 1992), as quoted in *Marriage Partnership*, summer 2003, 10.

## Chapter 14: I Don't Feel Like Submitting Today!

1. Leslie Vernick, *How to Act Right When Your Spouse Acts Wrong* (Colorado Springs, CO: WaterBrook, 2001), 27.
2. Gary Thomas, *Sacred Marriage: What If God Designed Marriage to Make Us Holy More than to Make Us Happy?* (Grand Rapids, MI: Zondervan, 2000).

## Chapter 17: Celebrating Each Other's Strengths

1. Glenn Zaephel, *He Wins, She Wins: Turn the Battle for Control in Your Marriage into a "Win-Win" Partnership* (Nashville, TN: Nelson, 1994), 124.
2. Gary Thomas, *Sacred Marriage: What If God Designed Marriage to Make Us Holy More Than to Make Us Happy?* (Grand Rapids, MI: Zondervan, 2000), 13.

# About the Author

DR. DEBBIE L. CHERRY is a licensed clinical psychologist, author, and speaker. She is the President/CEO of Today's Family Treasures (TFT), a ministry focused on restoring and revitalizing marriages and families. She serves as the lead psychologist for TFT's signature R&R program, devised to restore marriages in crisis, and is the featured speaker of TFT's "Unlocking the Treasure of Marriage" conferences. She also serves as the chief psychologist of Eaglecrest Counseling Center in Springfield, Missouri.

Dr. Cherry received her masters and doctoral degrees from Oklahoma State University, Stillwater, Oklahoma, and has been practicing in the Springfield, Missouri, area for the past fifteen years. She was instrumental in the development and organization of the Christian Mental Health Association for the Greater Springfield Region.

Dr. Cherry has authored or coauthored several books including: *Discovering the Treasure of Marriage* (Cook Communications/ Life Journey, 2003); *Feeding Your Appetites: Take Control of What's Controlling You* (Integrity Press, 2004); *Childproofing Your Marriage: Keeping your Marriage a Priority during the Parenting Years* (Cook Communications/Life Journey, 2004); and *Escaping the Parent Trap: 14 Principles for a Balanced Family Life* (Cook Communications/Life Journey, 2006).

She has been the featured guest on more than thirty radio programs across the nation including *Focus on the Family, Prime Time America, American Family Radio News, Faith to Action, Viewpoint,* and *Christian Interest News.* Her television appearances include *Total Living with Jerry Rose,* and *At Home Live.*

Dr. Cherry has been married for nineteen years. She and her husband, Jim, live in Springfield, Missouri, with their four children, Taffeta, Tiara, Talon, and Trayton.

CPSIA information can be obtained at www.ICGtesting.com
Printed in the USA
LVOW13s2014151213

365446LV00003B/61/P

"Dr. Debbie Cherry tackles one of the most misunderstood and touchy subjects among women today with sensitivity and wisdom. Debbie has done what few strong-willed women want to do: explore God's intent for marriage. As only a strong-willed wife herself could do, she challenges other strong-willed wives to be all God intended them to be both in and out of the marriage. Thank you, Debbie, for your boldness and vulnerability!"

—DR. TIM CLINTON, EdD, LPC, LMFT

"Being married to an amazingly godly and quite strong-willed woman, I have learned firsthand the struggles and wonderful blessings that come from a wife with those personality traits. Debbie Cherry has done an outstanding job of tackling this very sensitive topic that I believe can be addressed effectively only by a strong-willed woman. Debbie reaches the reader by her willingness to expose her own struggles with biblical submission within her marriage. Debbie Cherry provides a wonderful starting point for any strong-willed woman to learn how to balance her personality in such a way that it brings honor to both God and her husband."

—GARY SMALLEY, author of *I Promise*

"Debbie Cherry is an amazing writer. God's truth and Debbie's experiences in the trenches with people who struggle with the realities of life on a very common problem that is too often ignored. A strong-willed wife can either become an ungodly and desperate creature or a godly woman using all her gifts to create a life of meaning and purpose for herself, her husband, and her children. This book makes all the difference as to which way the force of the will is directed."

—STEVE ARTERBURN, author of *Every Man's Battle*
and *Healing Is a Choice*

"If you are a strong-willed Christian woman, this book is for you. Dr. Cherry practically presents how God's plan of submission is not just a necessary evil but also a blessing for your marriage. Her transparency and honesty as a strong-willed wife will remind you that you are not alone on this journey."

—JULIANA SLATTERY, author of
*Finding the Hero in Your Husband*

"This book draws you in—even if you're skeptical. Dr. Cherry provides a well-reasoned and compelling argument for what biblical submission should look like for both men and women. I can hardly wait to talk to her about it on the radio!"

—DAN ROBBINS, producer, Focus on the Family's
*Weekend Magazine*